Young Writers 2005 CREATIVE WRITING COMPETITION FOR SECONDARY SCHOOLS

T·A·L·E·S·

From West Midlands Vol III
Edited by Steve Twelvetree

Disclaimer

Young Writers has maintained every effort
to publish stories that will not cause offence.

Any stories, events or activities relating to individuals
should be read as fictional pieces and not construed
as real-life character portrayal.

 Young**Writers**

First published in Great Britain in 2005 by:
Young Writers
Remus House
Coltsfoot Drive
Peterborough
PE2 9JX
Telephone: 01733 890066
Website: www.youngwriters.co.uk

SB ISBN 1 84602 310 6

Foreword

Young Writers was established in 1991 and has been passionately devoted to the promotion of reading and writing in children and young adults ever since. The quest continues today. *Young Writers* remains as committed to engendering the fostering of burgeoning poetic and literary talent as ever.

This year, *Young Writers* are happy to present a dynamic and entertaining new selection of the best creative writing from a talented and diverse cross section of some of the most accomplished secondary school writers around. Entrants were presented with four inspirational and challenging themes.

'Myths And Legends' gave pupils the opportunity to adapt long-established tales from mythology (whether Greek, Roman, Arthurian or more conventional eg The Loch Ness Monster) to their own style.

'A Day In The Life Of ...' offered pupils the chance to depict twenty-four hours in the lives of literally anyone they could imagine. A hugely imaginative wealth of entries were received encompassing days in the lives of everyone from the top media celebrities to historical figures like Henry VIII or a typical soldier from the First World War.

Finally 'Short Stories', in contrast, offered no limit other than the author's own imagination while 'Hold The Front Page' provided the ideal opportunity to challenge the entrants' journalistic skills, asking them to provide a newspaper or magazine article on any subject of their choice.

T.A.L.E.S. From West Midlands Vol III is ultimately a collection we feel sure you will love, featuring as it does the work of the best young authors writing today.

Contents

Ashlawn School

Brooke School

Coundon Court School & Community College

Darren Jackson (14)	75
Jaspreet Shoker (14)	76
Rebecca Hitchings (14)	77
Leanne Pitt (14)	78
Stephen Harley (14)	79
George Tunnicliffe (13)	80
Matthew Parsons (13)	81
Rebecca Sweet (14)	82
Tom Bromley (14)	83
Adele Kenny (14)	84
Jake Bevan (13)	85
Jessica Moore (13)	86
Abdul Almajdub (14)	87
Laura Morton (14)	88
Tara Wilson (14)	89
Rebecca Dale (14)	90
Samantha Phillips (14)	91
Daniel Jelley (14)	92
Melody Hall (14)	93
Georgina Holt (13)	94
Steven James Du'Mont (14)	95
Liam Doyle (14)	96
Oliver Holmes (14)	97
Matthew Greenbank (14)	98
Alex Jones (14)	99
Jason Rogers (14)	100
Chanelle Collier (14)	101
Zoe Cluff (14)	102
Samantha Purcell (14)	103
Timothy Devenport (13)	104
Russell Hopkins (14)	105
Kelly O' Connor (13)	106
Matthew McFeely (14)	107
Adam Whittingham (14)	108
Katie Dadic (14)	109
Stacey Dodd (14)	110
Abbie Fellowes (14)	111
Chris Marchenko (14)	112
Danny Jones (14)	113
Sam Kiernan (13)	114

Hodge Hill Girls' School

Charlotte Rogers (12)	149
Claire King (13)	150
Samiya Hussain (12)	151
Faybian Taylor (12)	152
Atiyah Ghulam (12)	153
Priya Minhas (12)	154
Henna Aliya Hussain (12)	155
Asma Mahmood (13)	156
Amena Iqbal (13)	157
Sawera Bukhari (13)	158
Aisha Ghafoor (12)	159
Jessica Ahmed (12)	160
Sana Jamil (12)	161
Zakia Sultana (12)	162
Farhat Naeem (12)	163
Rukhsana Momotaj (12)	164
Harsimran Minhas (12)	165
Saima Jokhia (13)	166
Maryam Aziz (12)	167
Anisa Bi (12)	168
Azadi Mir (12)	169
Nadia Ali (13)	170
Lauren Elizabeth Daly (13)	171
Natalie Green (13)	172
Bethany Shannahan (11)	173
Rukhsar Asif	174
Samaira Begum (13)	175

Plantsbrook School

Matthew Urwin (15)	176
Jemma Stanley (14)	177
Samantha Johnson (14)	178
Josh Jones (14)	179
Jacob Pardoe (14)	180
Monique Watkeys (14)	181
Emily Ward (13)	182
Heather O'Brien (14)	183
Thomas Surridge (14)	184
Danielle Watkeys (14)	185
James Willis (14)	186

The Round Oak School & Support Service

The Creative Writing

Clone Wars

Once upon a time there was a man called Dr G. Dr G was a genius who invented many things until there was a war in his land.

Dr G had no army so he was a bit concerned; that's when an idea hit him. The idea was to clone himself by building a cloning machine.

He worked day and night until he built the cloning machine. Finally he cloned himself and started fighting back.

After Dr G's enemy found out what he was doing he decided to steal the machine and clone himself.

Dr G's enemy was called Black Cat; Black Cat chose to clone himself with the machine as well. It was obvious that Dr G was outnumbered.

Dr G and his army lost the war and they all died at the hands of Black Cat.

Tim Musumbu
Alumwell Business & Enterprise College

The Cellar

One dark night I was walking down the squeaky stairs when I saw a light. I wondered it if should check it out, but I did anyway. The light was coming from the cellar; I started to walk towards the cellar door when I suddenly felt some hands on me. I turned around and I saw two big, cold, hair-raising things. I tried to scream but the things put their hands over my mouth. The things said to me, 'Please don't scream. We don't want anyone to know that we're here.'

'Why? What are you doing here?' I asked.

'We've come to find a little girl named Samantha,' they said.

I was in shock when they said my name. 'My name is Samantha but everyone calls me Sam,' I cried.

'Well you have been chosen to be the knight, you have to save Princess Kari,' the things said.

Latrice Shannon (13)
Alumwell Business & Enterprise College

My Cellar

I had walked this way to school for two years and I'd never noticed the small door in the wall before. *Perhaps something had been in front of it,* I thought, *or perhaps I had been looking in the opposite direction.*

As I stepped out of the school's hallway into the dark, dim, unusual dimension, walking down the steps, it was cold and creepy. I was terrified and felt sluggish. It was too cold to bear but became more tranquil as I went into the darkness. I started to tremble as the dirty, crawly, creepy webs clipped me. I was feeling uncomfortable and wondered what was there. Feeling awkward I started to think, *is it just me or something else like . . . I don't know! . . .* Too scary to imagine.

'What's there? What is it?' Afraid of what I might see.

I pushed the broken door. In I went and saw a dark, quiet room, totally nothing except for a bookcase which held some spooky books. I touched a book and a key fell out leading to something secret. 'What does it belong to?'

Suddenly my eye spotted a lock beside the bookcase leading to another cellar. I went down 369 steps, I think (they seemed never-ending). Finally I reached the bottom. My blood started to turn cold; I then realised someone else was there with me. I said 'Hello, who's there?' I turned around and a *sparkle* went right through me leaving me with just *bones ... bones ... bones ... !*

Mehvish Imran (13)
Alumwell Business & Enterprise College

Untitled

I was tiptoeing through the corridor when I suddenly bumped into this historical, ancient door. Then I noticed this rusted door handle covered in webs. I was excited so I started going toward that very door when I heard a roar coming from the cellar.

I got scared but was still up to the challenge so I started to go down the steep stairs and suddenly saw a shadow. I got a broom and started to go further down the stairs and when I got to the bottom I saw that it was a small mouse's distorted shadow.

In the dim light I thought I saw a dead person. I froze, feeling empty inside but really it was a dog nibbling on a chicken bone. I gave a sigh of relief but then, all of a sudden, someone grabbed me by my throat …

Rakyab Ahmed (13)
Alumwell Business & Enterprise College

To Minehead Seaside

In June I went to a seaside town called Minehead. I went with my mum, my stepdad and my brothers. We went for a weekend and we stayed in a bed and breakfast. On the Saturday we went to the seaside and in the evening we had our dinner in a pub. Then we went back to the bed and breakfast. In the room that we had there was a double bed and bunk beds.

The next day we had a fry-up for breakfast and then we went to the beach. This time we went into the arcade and I won a lipgloss and a toe ring.

We went back to the bed and breakfast and got our stuff as it was time to go home. It took two hours and thirty minutes to get back home but when we arrived we all wished that we were still at Minehead seaside.

Still it was a fun weekend even if it was only for two days. At least we got to do things as a family and not individually. I liked it at Minehead seaside; it was a fun place to go as a family with lots of things you could do together.

Hannah Worton (11)
Alumwell Business & Enterprise College

The Journey Begins

'Hey, where's my MP3 player gone? I was listening to that yesterday and now it's gone,' I screamed.

'Go and look upstairs, it's probably on your shelf where you left it, knowing you,' said Mom.

'Got it!'

'See, I told you,' said Mom. 'Are you ready yet?'

'Mmmmmmm, na!'

'Well hurry up then!' yelled Mom.

'OK, OK, calm down. I'm done now anyway,' I was getting more and more excited by the minute.

'Right now, come on!' screamed Mom.

I finally reached school and all my friends were there waiting for me.

'Safe Jack,' Karl greeted.

'Safe Karl,' I replied. 'Can you wait to go on the cruise because I can't?'

'You're telling me, I just can't wait.'

All the mums were crying, especially mine; she had a big puddle on the floor next to her.

We were finally on the coach ready to go. We were going to be on the coach for four hours, unbelievable. Abid and I were sitting next to each other. We were good friends and I was missing my family already and we had only been gone for half an hour. As we were going along the motorway we adored the lovely green trees. They were beautiful.

We were finally there.

The SS Alumwell was enormous. I was worried at first. I didn't want to go on it just in case something went wrong. I sent a text to my mom to say I had arrived safely then I started crying. I was sad, but I was perfectly fine afterwards when the porters carried our bags onto the SS Alumwell.

'This ship is enormous, isn't it?' shouted Abid.

'Sure is,' said Karl

I was really looking forward to going on the cruise, I really was.

The cruise liner finally set sail. Karl, Abid and I looked for our cabin. It was massive. The beds were really comfortable. We all shared the room and it was great.

'Abid, Karl, stop eating all the food. You've eaten everything apart from one pizza and that's mine!'

'I feel sick,' said Karl.

'Me too,' replied Abid.

'What do you expect eating all the food? And what are you moaning at me for?'

We were on our way to the first country of the cruise, which was Florida. *Hooray!*

Jack Harding (12)
Alumwell Business & Enterprise College

The Cellar Of Evil

(An extract)

I was walking down the stairs step by step, getting nearer and nearer to the old cellar; it was dark as though the moon was covered with pitch-black clouds. I thought my vision was distorted when I saw a grave but when I rubbed my eyes and opened them, it was a grave! Suddenly I went as cold as ice, I felt that someone touched me so I turned around; I couldn't believe it, it was a ghost!

'Hello,' said the ghost, my name is Jack Linson and I like food, oh by the way, I ate your apple pie.'

'That's it, you're going down!' I shouted. I looked on the floor and I found a vacuum cleaner and sucked up the ghost.

'No!' shouted the ghost, but it was too late, the ghost had been sucked up.

I went back upstairs, step by step, my heart beating faster and faster. Finally I reached the last step of the old, crooked stairs. From out of thin air, a blaze of charming white light burst into my heart as if Cupid, the Greek god of love had shot an arrow of love into my heart. In front of me there lay a lady in bed whose beauty shone like the moon itself. She had shiny blonde hair as the sun itself and she was lying in a bed full of rose petals; her eyes was as the stars in Heaven, her skin was white as the clouds in paradise, her body was shaped as an angel. She spoke in a charming voice, 'Would you love me or sacrifice me?' said the mysterious gorgeous figure.

I walked towards the bed, knowing deep down in my heart that this was wrong but I couldn't resist her charming figure. I crawled onto the bed like a hungry beast wanting its prey. Now I lay on her right side beside the dagger. She grabbed my hands furiously, her charming face coming towards me and she tried to kiss me but I had a bad feeling, this was wrong, so as I started to kiss her I pushed her charming face away from me and I jabbed the dagger into her chest, piercing her heart.

Ahsun Saddique (13)
Alumwell Business & Enterprise College

Untitled

(An extract)

'Oh my God!' Tina woke up with a shudder. She got out of bed to reach for the water as her face sweated like an ocean. What did I see? Who was he? Was this a sign from God? Am I going to meet him? All these things rolled around Tina's head. She couldn't wait for the morning to come. As soon as the dawn lightened the sky, she phoned Eddie, her best friend.

'Hello, Eddie speaking,' he answered.

'Eddie, hi, it's me, Tina. Look, I've got to talk to you. Can we meet up before school? Wait for me near the canteen!'

Taking a breath, Eddie replied, wondering what she was on about. 'Okay, I will be there but what's wrong? Why does your voice seem shattered?'

'Nothing, I've got something important to tell you. Just turn up on time please.'

'Okay, I'll …' Eddie heard a loud bang! 'Hello? Hello? Tina, you still there?'

Tina got dressed as quickly as she could and stood outside the canteen at 8 o'clock. Meanwhile Eddie had just got out of the shower. Forgetting the time, he got dressed.

'Where's Eddie? He always does this, he is half an hour late.' Tina was fast losing patience, when all of a sudden Eddie's head popped from around a corner.

'I got here as fast as I could even though -'

'Shut up! Listen! Last night I had a dream. It was me, you and a guy -'

'W-w-wait a minute, you're meaning to say that you dragged me out of bed at 7 o'clock to tell me about a dream?' Eddie could not figure out what had got into Tina when she saw a guy …

Bismillah Aftab
Alumwell Business & Enterprise College

The Forbidden Cellar

(An extract)

I walked further and further into the dark cellar, the steps creaked and then I saw a dull light in the corner. I walked in further. There were no bags of anything down in the cellar but there was a trapdoor. I didn't know whether to go through it but suddenly the cellar door swung open and a voice from nowhere said, 'Enter!'

I stood there shocked, and again the voice said, 'Enter, enter, enter.'

I was so shocked that I slowly walked down into another cellar. There was a man sitting in a corner wearing a black cloak. He slowly turned round and said, 'Welcome, I'm sorry about the scare I gave you in the last cellar. Don't be scared because you and I have a lot of things in common. Let me ask you, did you know that I am your father?'

'No, you can't be my father, my father's upstairs,' I said.

The man in the cloak said, 'My name is Gordon and I am your father.'

'I am Patrick, your son, but where have you been all these years?'

Gordon said, 'I am a guardian of free will and one day, my son, you will be a guardian of free will. I made your parents into robots because I had to do a twelve-year mission.'

Sam Patten (13)
Alumwell Business & Enterprise College

It's Just A Dream

It was a very rainy morning and all the children were shivering and shaking. It was pouring down in gigantic water/ice drops; it was freezing.

Lightning; all the children screamed like scared howling dogs.

I was watching Miss, she was really scared but she pretended to be calm all the time. I was not a bit frightened, I was just watching the lightning bounce off the clouds from the classroom window. All the children were very quiet and looked like they had seen a ghost. They were all hiding underneath the classroom tables.

'What was that?' Miss screamed because the lights flickered on and off. You could tell she was really petrified. All I could see was the lightning flashes. The door flung open but there was nobody there …

The phone rang. Miss crawled over to it but nobody was there.

'Miss, help me please,' one of the children cried.

'What is it?' Miss said.

'Bubblegum has stuck to him. It must have been that new chewing gum that I stuck there this morning.'

'Wake up now, you're going to be late for school!' I woke up and my mom was angry with me; I was going to be late. Then I realised I had been dreaming but it was 9am, I was late …

Devina Patel (12)
Alumwell Business & Enterprise College

A Night Of The Shadows

It was one lonely night. I was lost. All the houses had disappeared into thin air. Suddenly I noticed there was a shadow following me. I turned around but no one was there. I was so suspicious that someone or something was following me so I turned around again and shouted, 'Who is there? Is someone following me?'

It was so quiet now. After a few minutes I could hear slow but loud footsteps. I looked sideways and I actually saw a shadow and it wasn't my imagination going wild! The shadow walked like a zombie towards me.

I ran as fast as I could to get away from the creepy shadow. I tripped over something which felt like stone. It was a gravestone and there were other gravestones everywhere! I finally found out where I was. It was the graveyard, which I knew wasn't a good place to be. I was so frightened! There was a house just a few metres away. I quickly ran to the safe house (as I called it). Inside it was very dark. I couldn't see a thing. Something wrapped around my legs. I was so frightened that I stopped breathing!

Madeen Saddique (12)
Alumwell Business & Enterprise College

Dafoe's Revenge

When Dafoe was young, his parents were killed. How did all this happen? I will tell you.

One bright, sunny day, Dafoe and his parents were going to Alton Towers; on the way Dafoe needed to go to the toilet so his dad took him and his mother waited in the car. When they came back, they found his mother gone, but they saw a note. Dad picked it up and it said: *'£25million to Black Ally House. Don't involve the police or the old woman will die!'* Dad was shocked and cried, 'What will we do?'

Next day, they took and money and suddenly they heard a voice,

'Put the money in the elevator and come up the stairs.'

When they got there they saw Mum tied up. Dad shouted, 'Let her go!'

Two men came from behind and tied him up too. One man gave a gun to Dafoe and he started his lecture. 'I'm the one who got your mom kidnapped. When I went to the toilet I called my bad friends to take the old woman away; I'm the one who wrote the note, I'm the one who wanted the money so when you die I can enjoy my life.'

'Why did you do this?' shouted Dad.

'It was my revenge for how you treated me. One little mistake and a smack in the head.'

Just as he was about to pull the trigger, the police came and took him away and he spent the rest of his life in prison.

Junaid Salloo (13)
Alumwell Business & Enterprise College

The Big Fight

I was walking down the stairs to the cellar, step by step, and had nearly reached the bottom when I heard a sound coming from somewhere. I turned around, but there was nothing there. Then suddenly in front of me stood a distorted ghost. When I got closer I saw it was an old cloth over a coat hanger.

Then out of nowhere a ghost appeared. It was as though possessed for a few seconds. Then a devil came out of the ground and said, 'You are going down, Lula Vanatine.'

The ghost said, 'No, you mean the opposite way round. You're going back down where you came from.

I was afraid when I realised this was a war between ghosts and devils. I sat on the step and saw lots of ghosts from the ceiling and lots of devils to support Lulu Vanatine and Tu Ake.

I was shocked, I couldn't believe my eyes! Then the fight began; ghost, Lulu Vanatine vs devil, Tu Ake. I didn't know why they were fighting but it was cool; there were punches and kicks flying, the devil was losing for a minute then he poked Lulu Vanatine in the eye who went crying to his supporters. The winner was the devil, Tu Ake. I was amazed, I thought I was dreaming but no, I wasn't.

The devil came closer and closer to me until he was right up to my face and he said, 'What is your name, kid?'

I replied, 'Jack, Sir.'

The devil said, 'By the way, I broke your bike.'

I said, 'That's it, you're dead!'

The devil replied, 'Bring it on.'

The fight began, I punched him and kicked away his stick that he had poked the ghost with. The devil went flying into the wall and I chucked the devil into the hole and said, 'You're down!'

The ghosts were so proud of me that they fixed my bike and I was very, very grateful.

Arian Cani (13)
Alumwell Business & Enterprise College

The Animals That Escaped

I was walking into a creepy old cellar. I went through the door and down the stairs. I heard a noise as I entered the cellar. Suddenly the lights went dim. My vision was distorted. Everything was as dark as the midnight sky. I could see something but couldn't make out what it was.

I carried on going down the stairs and I saw a gorilla. He was huge and he had escaped from the zoo. He was very angry. I called the zookeepers and they came immediately. They grabbed the gorilla to take him back to the zoo but he didn't fit in the car so they got a van and took him back to the zoo. Then suddenly I found a tiger, some lions and all kinds of animals in the cellar; it was like a zoo. All the animals were fighting. I called the zoo and asked if they had lost any more animals and they said, 'Yes.'

I said, 'I think I've got them over here.'

The zookeepers said, 'OK, we'll be over right away,' and they came and had to fight the animals in order to capture them. Eventually they captured them all and I got £500 reward.

Naveed Aslam (13)
Alumwell Business & Enterprise College

Sea Creatures

It all started when we went back to school. It was the second lesson and it was boring science. Every kid always asked the teacher if we were going on a trip and the answer was always, 'No!' so every lesson was the same, always about sea creatures.

Miss Brett was always explaining and giving detentions out until one day the head teacher came and said that Year 7 had been doing a lot about sea creatures (he could say that again! I mean every day learning about sea creatures!). He carried on and said he had some exciting news. Some of Year 7 kids would be going on a trip under the sea. Everyone got excited and he called out some names and me, Neelam, Sanya, Sabeeya and Samina were chosen, all of us from Year 7. He said that we would be leaving the next morning and must pack our stuff. He gave us permission slips to bring back with us.

The next day we put all of our stuff in a submarine and said goodbye to our families. While we were going down through the water we saw a squid swimming near us. Neelam and Samina were scared and Sanya felt sick. Subeeya and I just sat there. We took pictures of sharks as they looked right at us. They were hungry! Suddenly something got on top of the submarine. It was a slimy octopus. You could see his legs.

We spent three great days under the sea watching the fascinating life of sea creatures.

Naila Dad (12)
Alumwell Business & Enterprise College

Tales

I dived in. I went quite far down. I saw the button on the side. I'd never seen it before. I'm normally in the top group but I was showing Group 3 how to dive. It looked unusual as it was red and shiny. I told my mate and I took her down with me. She thought it was a plug but I didn't.

The bell rang to tell us the lesson was over. I heard some people laughing behind the changing room door. I got scared. I was on my own. I decided to follow the sound and it led me to the red button but then it disappeared. I went home and I wrote about it in my diary.

I woke up in the morning and I went to school early to go back to the red button in the pool. It was still there and so was the laugh; I hadn't imagine it. I unscrewed the red button; there was a deep hole. I sent my gerbil through the hole and he was gone for ages. I started to get worried but when he came back he looked like he had had a good time. I told Miss Stokes and she didn't believe me. She thought I was going loopy.

I told the Head of Year and I showed him. He saw it and laughed. I said, 'Why are you laughing?' He said that the laughing was coming from the caretaker's room. Mr Ben showed me and I couldn't believe it.

I told everyone but I saved the day because there was a hole in the side and the caretaker's room was flooding. I got a merit and a certificate. Mr Ben said, 'Well done!' so now I'm head of the Leadership Council.

Charlie Foster (11)
Alumwell Business & Enterprise College

The Journey Begins

'Mom, where's my other trainers?' I shouted in distress and, not getting a reply, I decided to find something to cheer me up. I thought my mind was in two worlds. My older sister was blasting her music enough to wake the dead! My little brother was throwing action figures about, distraught, and there's me in the middle of the room, half naked ... *half naked!*

I raced about to find something decent to wear, dragging stuff out of my closet backwards. *Zzzzzzzz!* After ten minutes of non-stop packing, I had finally finished.

'Ryan, come on now, we're going.'

'What about my hair?' I replied.

'Put a hat on then,' Mum bawled.

I slowly stumbled down the stairs and bounced over the stair gate but then realised that I didn't want to go, I tried to find an excuse, *'Mmmm,* I need the toilet.'

'Ryan, no, use the ones at school and let's be off,' Mom replied in an exhausted manner.

'I'll ... *mmm,* OK,' but I didn't really mean that, so as slowly as possible I dawdled over towards my mom's car; I was just trying to waste time, tying my shoelace as my mom threw me into the car and strapped my seatbelt around me.

It was a nail-biting ride. As we arrived, the ship looked gigantic and a glistening white caught the corner of my eye, on which was carved in black ink, *SS Alumwell.* My mom was speechless.

As I took a few steps towards the ship I spotted my best friend Daljit running towards the cruise liner. I bawled, 'Daljit, Daljit, come this way.' He turned in joy and made his way towards me.

As I grabbed my stuff and followed Daljit towards the ship, it brought a tear to my mom's eye ...

Ryan Bethell (12)
Alumwell Business & Enterprise College

The Trees

I had walked this way to football for three years and I'd never seen the big, massive trees on the left-hand side of the main road. Perhaps I had always got my head in the clouds or I had just never looked over the road before. I took no more notice and carried on walking to football, which was just behind the trees. I got my boots and kit on and was ready to play when I had a flashback. I remembered that a man was pushing a woman into the trees. I had a cold shiver down my spine. *Aah!* While I was playing football I could hear screaming and shouting for ages.

I started walking home and it was like Tony Blair had been shot; hundreds and thousands of police cars were on the left-hand side of the road where the trees were. I was getting anxious, there was a puddle of blood on the ground and what looked like a member of the woman's family. I started to feel as though I was in a sauna, sweating like a farm pig. I started to run home.

When I turned the corner I bumped into an old man but I carried on running; nothing was stopping me.

I got home and I slammed the door open and fled up the stairs, running like a cheetah. I tried to go to sleep but I couldn't; it was making me feel sick as if my belly was like a whirlpool churning. My mom came up to bring me a glass of water and she said, 'Whatever is the matter James?' I didn't reply and pretended I was asleep.

I woke up the next morning and went to football again but this time I went another way there. I played the same and nothing felt wrong but at half-time I was going to the changing room for a team talk and I heard someone shout, 'James, come here!' It was the police. All I could feel was a big lump in my throat like I had swallowed a brick. I ran over to them while everyone was watching and they said, 'You are coming downtown, Sonny Jim.' I thought to myself, *they are going to blame me,* but all they wanted was to ask some questions. While I was in there they showed me pictures of the crime scene and said I was seen as a witness by the old man I'd knocked over . . .

James Lowbridge (12)
Alumwell Business & Enterprise College

The Queen's Robots!
(An extract)

There was a war about to happen, people were talking about it saying that robots were going to take over, but still no one listened. No one listened to me, why? They should have listened, they would not now all be in a cave under the earth starving to death. Only once a week they get fed. I don't think they even get fed that much.

Well, I will tell you something. I am not trapped down there starving to death. Oh no! I am on Earth surviving with food and water and sometimes haunted by *them*. *Them* are horrible things. Even though they are just robots you will not believe me if I tell you what they did to some poor, poor girl. Oh no, you will think I am mad. They use your insides as things to charge themselves, but they do not always have to use people's insides to keep alive; they do not have to do that, no no; they used to use chargers to charge themselves, but then one day, something bad happened; something so bad that every night I have nightmares that we are going to relive the war and how the war happened.

Well, I will have to tell you so you can understand what position these people are in and the position I am in.

One night, as normal, all the robots went to get charged; to the robots it is going to sleep, so one night when we all put the robots on charge, a robot got unplugged and was kind of experimented on. A great scientist was trying to see if robots were capable of solving things themselves and if they were able to do things for themselves and if they could have a mind of their own. Well, I bet you can guess what happened next - the robots thought that people, humans, were very bad health to the world and so they thought that they should put humans under the earth because humans were very bad for the Earth, well, according to the robots they were, so there was a war. Humans thought that robots should be destroyed so humans fought back, but humans lost the war. I told them. I told them all that we were going to fail the war and that the robots were too strong but did they listen? No!

No they did not. The Queen said that the robots were not clever enough to develop a war against humans; the Queen said that humans made the robots clever just to clean and ride people about and to go shopping for people as slaves, but I said there was someone else involved, a human, a *great* scientist who was cleverer than anyone in the world, his name was James, Sir James ...

Simmone Austin (14)
Alumwell Business & Enterprise College

The Big Race

The deadline was four months away and it had become very urgent for my friend Faris and I to get our transport sorted out for the big race.

So Faris and I went back to our huge garage called FO Cars. But we thought we hadn't a good enough car to win so we went to our friend, Selector, to check what he had. We went to the back of the yard and that's when we found a rusty old Subaru; the engine wasn't working so we took it to a place called 'Pimp My Ride' which customised cars. We told them what we wanted ... a nitro car sprayed dark blue with phoenix-yellow colour stickers, black leather seats in the interior, TV in the headrest, black front spoilers, 19-inch gold rims, V9 engine and blue rear spoilers. We were amazed, we couldn't believe how brilliant it looked but the problem was, the car was too expensive, £4,000, so we made a bet that if we won the race we didn't have to hand over any money but if we lost they could have the car for free.

It was the day of the race. The horn blew and the raced started. I was doing the first lap with an extraordinary speed of 230mph. We were going so fast that the wheels were eating up the dirt. Ahead there was a bridge, 8ft long and we were in fourth place. I got angry and put the nitro on. The car jumped over the bridge and we ...

Qasim Naveed (12)
Alumwell Business & Enterprise College

Deep In The Bottom Of The Ocean

(An extract)

'Well, Papa, I just want to see the wonders of the ocean. Please! Please let me go, I promise I'll come back in a short while and I won't let anyone see me,' said Hoor, desperate to go up to the great stones.

'Yes dear, I can let you go but it's your mother. She's rather worried that you'll get into danger,' her father said.

It's Mother's fault you're saying dear?' said Sana, the king's wife and queen of the deep in the bottom of the oceans. The queen and the great king had their own powers but in the deep sea, they could only be used when needed.

The king and queen had a little chat and decided to let Hoor go up. 'Raja, are you sure she'll, be fine?' the queen said.

'Yes dear, she's eighteen, she can protect herself,' said the King.

Up in the world, the little mermaid was humming, *'Hummmlalalala.'* The mermaid looked very happy as she sang but her sweet voice reached the bad wolf gang in their seabed and went all the way down the palace of the king and queen. They sat together and listened to the sweet hum. 'Oh, doesn't she have a sweet voice?' said the queen proudly.

'Yes, yes, it is very nice, in fact it's beautiful,' said the king with a star of joy on his face, as in a big smile.

'I am enjoying it, it's like, well, I can't really explain it,' said the queen.

'Well, I think our daughter has the gift of singing, don't you?' said the King.

'Yes,' answered the queen.

The bad wolf got his gang together and they caught the princess in a net. She screamed, *'Argh!'* The king and queen heard her voice and swam to her as fast as they could. When they reached the top there was a splash … !

Ghosia Shahid (12)
Alumwell Business & Enterprise College

Nightmare On Elm Street
And Alien Vs Predator

One cold and stormy night on Elm Street, a boy called John was doing his routine, walking the dog. He always walked the dog around the block. However, one night Jonny approached John and struck him using all his force with a hammer. John fell to the ground and that was when Jonny pulled out his sword and cut him up. That was where the trouble started; the dog started to bark at Jonny and that made Jonny very, very mad. He picked up the dog and threw it over the fence. That was not a very nice scene! Jonny picked up the pieces of the body and returned back to base.

At the base Jonny had a look at some of the pieces and placed them on his face. After that he went hunting once more but not just for one person, about 25 people exactly. It was quite easy because they were all on one coach. As Jonny approached the coach he spotted something in the sky. It was an alien spaceship preparing to land. Jonny thought nothing of it. He carried on when suddenly he saw another ship, but this looked like a predator's ship and that was when he worried. The ships plunged to the ground. He went to see what was happening. There were aliens and predators fighting. For some reason they all stopped and then started again but this time Jonny was involved …

Josh Seva (11)
Alumwell Business & Enterprise College

The Journey Begins!

'Mom, have you washed my pink top?' I shouted from upstairs.

'It's in your wardrobe,' said Mum, as she came upstairs into my bedroom.

'What about my new jeans?' I asked.

'They're in your pink bag,' Mum replied.

I started packing my bag while Mom made my breakfast. I was getting excited as it got nearer the time to leave. I wanted to ring Harvinder but I thought, knowing her, she would still be asleep so I just carried on packing my clothes. I came downstairs, had my breakfast and got ready to go to school.

'Look after yourself,' Mom shouted.

'I will, bye, hurry up Dad,' I shouted.

When I got to school I saw Kiran and Anisha, they waved at me and I went running to catch them up.

'Hi, Farrah, I'm so excited I can't wait to go on the cruise,' Anisha said.

'I know, it's going to be really good,' Kiran said.

'Shall we go and sit inside the coach?' I asked.

'Yeah, let's go,' Anisha shouted.

We went and sat inside the coach; it had red curtains and a coffee machine. We arrived at the SS Alumwell; it was massive, bigger than the school!

'Everybody come in and give your bag to the porters,' Dr Dowd said.

'This is going to be really good, we don't even have to carry our bags,' I said.

'Look at the cabins, shall Farrah, Anisha, Kiran and I share a cabin, Sir?' asked Harvinder.

'Yes,' said Dr Dowd.

'Check out the bathroom, it's got a hairdryer, a shower and a bath,' I said.

'I'm sleeping on the second bunk bed,' Anisha said.

Farrah Mahmood (12)
Alumwell Business & Enterprise College

The Haunted House
(An extract)

There in front of me I saw a peculiar-looking object. It was as though that house was haunted but why was it haunted? What was wrong with it? I'll tell you the story.

Brrrng! The bell went and it was deafening. *'Huh!'* I said, my eyes accurately focusing on a large lady with the thickest glasses ever. They were so big that they covered the whole of her scary, fat face. 'Stop sleeping in my classroom!' She shouted so loudly that if you were in the corridor you could still hear her. I'm telling you frankly, the whole place boomed as well as her.

Oh no, I must have taken a slight nap. Okay, maybe not. But I can't help it; this lesson is so boring.

Calmly the tomato-faced, sharp-faced teacher said, 'As I was just explaining, we are going on an adventure.'

'Huh,' I spat out.

'I mean a school trip and you shouldn't talk to a teacher like that.'

While the teacher blabbered on about the 'adventure', something caught my eye. I glanced out of the window and out of the corner of my eye I saw something spooky!

Just then … 'Sarah Jane, are you listening to what I said?'

'Um … yeah!'

'Then tell me,' screamed the teacher.

'Well,' I stuttered …

'Oh, forget it I said we were going there …'

Everyone followed Mrs Flies' long finger to the window and then they looked out to see the spooky thing. 'Mrs … that's spooky …' I said like I was a baby.

'Oh, for goodness sake, it is not scary, it is a bright and nice place.'

'Oh for goodness sake, it is a scary place, a very dull, ugly place,' I said to myself quietly …

Shivani Pushkarna (12)
Alumwell Business & Enterprise College

The Cellar

(An extract)

I walked down the stairs, it was dark and it smelled like hot chilli Doritos. I heard a creak, it was the door. I felt for a light and I touched a furry little thing. It was a gremlin! It picked my fingernails and then it said, 'I want my mommy.' I laughed. The gremlin said, 'There is a monkey in the cellar and it is big and hairy.'

I heard a sudden movement, I turned around but it was distorted. I couldn't see anything. I said to the gremlin, 'If you are playing tricks on me, stop it because it's freaking me out!' I couldn't see anything except for a small, tiny, minuscule rat. I screamed and ran behind a box trying to evade it but then I looked at the box again and it said, 'Alex'. No one in this house is called Alex ... !

I unlocked the box and I saw a nasty, smelly, dirty sheet of paper. The paper had a dolly attached to it and it read, 'Do not read'. I thought, *should I read it or not?* I was eager to read it, so I did ...

Jasmine Chambers (13)
Alumwell Business & Enterprise College

The Demon Headmaster

(Based on 'The Demon Headmaster' by Gillian Cross)

I used to live in a foster home until I was finally fostered by the Millers. Mr and Mrs Miller had two boys called Harvey and Harry.

It was my last day at Oak Valley. I had said all my goodbyes. My social worker had arranged for me to go straight after school. I was going to stay with them and start my new primary school. (I was nervous.)

When I finally got there I was quiet. Harvey and Harry invited me upstairs; they offered me all sorts of snacks but I refused. Their favourite programme was on, 'Zap!' It was all about monsters and zombies. They were both astonished that I hadn't heard of it. I told them that I wasn't into that sort of thing.

After breakfast, I nearly forgot that Mum had written me a letter explaining that I was new and I hadn't got the school uniform. When we were talking at school, Harvey told me about the headmaster and how mean he was.

When I entered the gate, there were bizarre groups of people who were answering questions on different topics. Two Year 9 pupils came and everyone got in lines. I was standing there when one of them yelled, 'Who are you?'

I showed the letter and she shouted, 'Go and see the headmaster immediately!'

When I knocked at the headmaster's door and then slowly entered, he said in a deep voice, 'Sit down Miss Banks.'

'Thank you, Headmaster.'

The spooky headmaster gave me a test. It was hard but I had already done this one before in my primary school. After the test the headmaster spooked me out; he had rays coming from his eyes. 'Look into my eyes deeply, you're very, very sleepy, you are going to fall asleep.' When I woke up, he told me that I had fallen asleep but that could not have been true as I went to bed at 8.30pm. He told me I should go to bed earlier.

He was a hypnotist!

Harvinder Aujla (12)
Alumwell Business & Enterprise College

My Tale Beyond The Mirror

I hate that mirror, I thought to myself. I have hated it ever since we moved into this house. I opened my eyes in the opposite direction of the mirror. Since I was little I have been scared of mirrors. I think it was after watching a horror movie about vampires. Anyway, tonight was the night I faced my fears. I rolled over and stared at the mirror.

It was glowing a vivid red. Suddenly it changed to a fluorescent purple then to silver and rapidly back to the vivid red. I stumbled towards it; my hand foolishly touched the surface but instead of the cold, smooth surface, it was warm and felt as if water was woven into the surface of it. It wasn't a liquid but it also wasn't a solid. I stood there for a second deciding whether it was solid or liquid. I could put my hand through the material. I glanced once more at my bedroom and then walked through the material! I felt like I was a gas floating freely around.

Suddenly, I was back in my bedroom again. I looked carefully around my room and spotted my calendar on the wall. It was the 22nd March instead of the 21st. I must have gone forward in time. I looked up; there was my real bedroom as big as a postage stamp. I wished I were back in 'my' room. Immediately I was back in my room, so suddenly that I fell over.

From then on I visited my time machine every night to see what would happen next, and guess what? I'm not scared of mirrors now!

Emily Gwilt (11)
Alumwell Business & Enterprise College

Jack's Revenge

Hu-hu-hu. My breath was panting, my heart was beating fast. I ran out of the house like the wind and not a gentle wind, a tornado! My friend Simon had disappeared into the darkness as I left him behind outside the house. The house was inhabited by a boy, soon to be a man with no mom or dad. They said he was the Devil's son and he had come to kill.

'No!' I heard a loud scream. It was Simon; he had just moved here two days ago and he was my only mate. I had no other friends and now Simon had been slain!

A day later I woke up in the house with blood all around me. I didn't know where it had come from and a shiver trickled down my spine. I ran out of the house, but with nowhere to go and no mother or father, I realised the house was where I had to stay; I was soon to be a man.

The ghosts in this house don't stop killing. I don't ever know what happened the night before I became possessed. I try not to see anyone in the night. My name is Jack and I am getting revenge for my parents. Everyone else has parents. I kill in the night and prey in the day. Now I know where the blood came from when I woke up. It was Simon's!

Anzal Ali (12)
Alumwell Business & Enterprise College

Opposite Life

One terrifying night a normal family was sound asleep. Four deadly burglars broke into Ashley Mango's house, the richest person in the world. Ashley Mango had the best security system in the world. The burglars were Fred Charles, David, Emmanuel and Soheel.

These burglars were wanted in all the countries in the world but that was not strictly true; the four deadly burglars were wanted in the evil world because they were agents and Ashley Mango was wanted around the world by the police. These agents were trying to prove Ashley Mango wrong. He had stolen from every country but made everybody believe that he was good and the burglars were evil. It took a whole year to get one piece of proof.

Two days later the agents were attacked by Ashley Mango's best henchmen. It was the DNA proof that the agents wanted.

They were on their way to Ashley Mango's house and very nearly got hit by bullets and they were out for revenge. They sneaked past the cameras and killed Ashley Mango's wife. This was serious. You could hear *broooof* in every room. They went to the master room and they shot Ashley.

Fred-Charles Pieterse (12)
Alumwell Business & Enterprise College

Water World

I will be going to Water World on the 15th July. We shall be leaving school at 9.30am and coming back at 6pm. When we go to Water World we will have to change into our swimming costumes and then we will be ready to go on the rides and have fun. We will be going on the slides and on the rapids. We will be going in a pool and we will be swimming around and we will be having lots of fun. We will also be going down other sides, doing backstroke and front stroke, swimming underwater and learning how to swim better.

We will be having lots of fun at Water World.

Sabrina Marsh (12)
Alumwell Business & Enterprise College

Our Day Out In The Safari Park

It took us half an hour to get to the safari park. When we got there we had to drive the car around in there. We saw lots of animals there. It was a very hot day. We took our own food and after a while I felt sick. When we ate we had to sit down.

There were lots of animals like monkeys, lions and elephants. I was still feeling sick so we had to sit in the car. When we drove past the animals they looked like they were going to come inside the car and the monkeys definitely wanted to get in. The doors were locked but they nearly broke the doors' handles. Then we parked up and I went and bought some sweets and drinks.

After a while we went to another part of the park where we saw some white tigers. My baby brother got scared and cried, and my dad was driving slowly because the tigers were walking in front of the car. My dad's car was scratched from top to bottom.

On the way back home I went to sleep in the car because I was very tired and I also had a headache. As soon as we got home we went to bed.

Shazad Shafa (12)
Alumwell Business & Enterprise College

A Story Of Strange Events

(An extract)

'Here it is! The waterfall of Angeron!' White water raced down like thundering horses; an impenetrable liquid curtain. Sala turned to Keif and murmured, 'Just through here.'

The expedition was nearly complete. The cave which they had all been seeking lay beyond the wall of water. Aral was the first to enter. His body lingered in the visible world for only a few seconds before it was swallowed, engulfed into the black vortex that lay beyond. It was undoubtedly eerie - a whole life vanishing before your eyes. Keif and Sala eagerly followed, leaving Meyer to enter alone. The ceaseless pounding of the water raged around him; an incessant suffocating weight upon him. Just as his very bones seemed to dampen, the air became cool and dry: safety.

The cave was dark - not the type of darkness that merely petrifies the body, but a shade of darkness that whispers fear to the soul and eats away at the song of confidence.

The rest of the group was already hidden in the depths of the labyrinth, frantically searching for the prize. Silence echoed and draped itself around them like an unwanted cloud. Just when the silence began to numb Meyer's mind and cause his heart to lurch ...

'Here,' breathed Sala, if such a tone or rich wonder may be called a breath, 'this is the stone of Zores!' Clutched in his hands, made grimy by the long journey, was an unremarkable red stone. It glowed with a dull red lustre - blood-glinting, it seemed.

'The secret to eternal life!' Sala added, his eager breath steaming the stone's surface. Keif reached out a claw-like hand to touch and caress. Suddenly, Sala's eyes turned cold and began to glint cruelly ...

Caroline Wood (14)
Arden School

Inside I'm Just Like You

Every day I sit in the same simple room. I never move. I'm a prisoner in my own body. The walls close in on me as my soul suffocates and dies. Every day they talk to me patronisingly until I am sure my heart will burst with the sheer effort of screaming at them. Of course, they cannot hear me. They will never hear me. They touch me but I cannot flinch, nor even feel their touch. I feel nothing except hatred for fate and for God, who let this happen to me. I am far away from life. And love. And hope. I am nought but a name, if that, an insignificant speck in a universe of vast disappointment. My life is meaningless, pointless and eternal. I seem immortal, for my incessant suffering never ceases. The world to me is like an empty void, endlessly and slowly spinning in time. Bittersweet dreams drift further away as I swipe hopelessly at them, a cat's paw in a mouse hole. Days merge into years as the world ages. I know not of the time; I know only of emptiness.

Despite this, I can think normally. This is the only device I have. Inside I'm just like you. Inside, I can dance and sing and laugh. Inside, I chatter loquaciously to myself. Just like you. Be thankful for what you have; you have a life.

Noise, on the stairs. The family, my family, is coming. To stare. At the invalid. Again.

Helen Roberts (13)
Arden School

The Dead Sea

There was an eerie dusk on the still water. The crescent moon was hidden behind the drifting, dreary clouds and only flickers of light succeeded in worming their way through them. The water was lifeless; a single pebble that lay beneath the motionless waves had more existence than that of the water itself.

A diminutive, gnarled rowing boat cut its way silently through the water. It lapped up against the weather-beaten wood and seeped down the side like rain trickling down a window on a gloomy day. The boat paddled on well into the night. The clouds became more threatening; they were like monsters bearing down on the boat, waiting to attack.

In the boat sat a hooded figure. She did not know where she was going, only that she had to reach the other side of the sea. She was running away from her miserable life back home and hoped there'd be something better awaiting her on the other side. Her long black hair was knotted and felt terrible because of the sea salt. Her eyes were so beautiful, yet her fringe shadowed them. Her clothes were rags, embedded with dirt and punctured with holes. The inner beauty of her was disguised by her outer appearance.

Crack! A lightning bolt pierced the sky breaking the far from peaceful silence. It was then the torrential rain began pounding down, little spirals in the water erupting all around her. The boat began to fiercely rock from side to side. It was swaying like a swing, only it was far from fun.

She began to paddle madly. Her vision was blurred and she had no idea whether her efforts were taking her backwards, forwards or in some other, unpredictable direction. She became breathless, panicked, scared; she no longer had any control. The waves were as big as mountains. They were charging at her like horses charging at one another in a medieval battle. The massive waves effortlessly swallowed up the boat.

She plunged into the ice-cold water. Her whole body felt as if it were being stabbed with razor-sharp knives. She took one final gasp of breath before her head became submerged under the inky blackness. Her vision was gone, yet she could see some kinds of figures floating around before her. She tried to reach out but could not summon the required energy. Her muscles were on fire, her head was pounding like an overpowering drum. She felt her last breath escape her; the bubble floated up through the water, so slowly, so calmly. It seemed unreal.

Her hands fell beside her. Her eyes closed, her head lolled to one side; she'd finally reached the other side of the sea.

Sarah Hunter (14)
Arden School

A Day In The Life Of My Dog Izzy

Izzy was just lying outside, minding her own business in the shade. Then she smelt something so she went and dug it up. She was there for 2 hours, made a huge hole and all there was to see was an old smelly glove. Then she got bored and went to sleep for another 2 hours.

The owner walked up to Izzy and said, 'Walkies.' As soon as they got out the back gate, Izzy shot down the back path because she'd seen a rabbit. The rabbit was gone though and Izzy was now lost. Then she went into a field and went to sleep for another 2 hours.

Izzy then woke up and another dog started walking beside her, Izzy started barking viciously. The dog barked back. A fight had broken out.

It was a stand-off, as though they were fighting each other for something. The other dog was a lot stronger. It snapped at her. Blood was pouring out, Izzy lost the fight. The other dog walked off and he was saying to Izzy, 'Easy, easy, easy.'

Izzy was dying and then she was dead.

David Dudgeon (12)
Ashlawn School

A Cat's Life

One morning, Tibbles the cat woke up. He went outside and saw some of his mates, Snowball and Fizz.

'Safe Fizz, safe Snowball.'

'You'll never guess who me and Snowball have just saw.'

'Who?'

'Lolly, Dash and Drifter.'

'You're joking.'

'No.'

Later on that day, Tibbles, Fizz and Snowball were down Featherbed Lane and so were Lolly, Dash and Drifter. 'Look,' said Fizz, 'there's Lolly, Dash and Drifter.'

Fizz, Snowball and Tibbles the leader of the Tibbles mafia, walked past Lolly, Dash and Drifter.

'Where are you three going?' said Lolly, the leader of the Lolly mafia.

'What's it got to do with you?'

'Nothing.'

Then something weird happened. Lolly, Dash and Drifter jumped Tibbles, Fuzz and Snowball. Tibbles turned and scratched Lolly right on his face, Lolly was lying on the ground. Dash and Drifter took on three of the strongest cats ever and Fizz took out two pistols and shot Dash and Drifter in the legs.

'Well done Fizz, great shooting,' said Tibbles.

The next morning, Tibbles and the rest went outside. Dash, Drifter and Lolly were there. 'What do you want?'

'Nothing, we just wanted to call it quits, yeah?' said Lolly.

'We're not that stupid.'

'Fine.' Lolly did this weird whistle and an army of cats stood behind him. 'Don't mess with the Lolly mafia.'

Then all these cats suddenly were stood behind Tibbles and all of them had machine guns and they shot Lolly's Mafia.

Philip Haworth (11)
Ashlawn School

Deathtrap Dungeon

The town of Fang was always quiet, but all that changed when an evil sorcerer named Melucio built a castle on the outskirts. He named it Deathtrap Dungeon. He filled this castle with malice, demons and traps. But by far the most terrifying thing was Belcon, the shape-shifting, fire-breathing dragon. There were vast riches up for grabs for anyone foolish enough to venture in there.

Fifty years passed and everybody who went in never came back out. But Kusko was determined to conquer the evil dungeon. He put on his chain mail, picked up his sword and ventured in. The corridors were dark and cold.

He heard a noise and stopped. Suddenly arrows flew out of both sides. He picked up two shields that were on the floor and ran through, blocking the arrows with the shields. He got to the end and heard groaning. He took out his sword. He noticed something sprawled on the floor. It wasn't a monster - it was a human. 'My name is Henry,' said the man, 'Belcon attacked me!'

Kusko helped him up and they ventured on. Suddenly the two men were surrounded by black knights who were possessed by Belcon. Kusko drew his sword and blocked the knights' attacks, hitting them back until they were dead. Kusko and Henry carried on to Belcon's domain. They went in and saw nothing, until Kusko turned round not to see Henry but a fifty-foot dragon.

'Foolish mortal,' said Belcon. 'I am a shape-shifter! I transformed into Henry to lure you here. Now I'm going to kill you!'

It breathed out fire but Kusko dodged it. Then Belcon scratched Kusko round the face but Kusko threw his sword right between its eyes. All the riches appeared and he magically disappeared out of the dungeon with them. He had conquered Deathtrap Dungeon.

Alistair Ferguson (12)
Ashlawn School

The Legend Of Giro's Shack

Fifty years ago in the small town of Portreath, Giro Stock, a boy of 12 with blond hair and glasses, came up with the idea of opening his own 'Surf Shack'. Now that he was 18, with years of surfing experience, he thought that today was the day. He propped up some bamboo canes against a brick wall and started creating this shop, shack, den - whatever you want it to be called. A couple of weeks later, it was finished. Surfboards ready to sell, wax ready to be bought.

Everyone in Portreath stuck together, Giro was like a celebrity with his surfing. But one horrific day this would change. Giro's first day of business had gone well, but a week into business the surfing channel in the shop was interrupted by the weather. *Freak Tidal Waves Approaching Newquay!*

Now, Portreath wasn't that far from Newquay, but it stuck into the sea more. Five minutes later, Portreath was empty except for some surfers and residents who didn't have time to leave. Portreath was quite a likely target, so pebbles were made into barriers on the shore. Hours later, Portreath fell silent. They could hear, see and feel the wave coming. Giro had no news of this, for he had been getting something from the storeroom when they had interrupted the surfing channel.

A total of 40 people were left in Portreath, 41 including Giro, but only one person knew he was there.

The waves were crashing into the stone barrier. They had to flee, so everyone ran to their cars and drove off. Giro came out the door and was taken down by pebbles, water and sand. All that was left was the chain on his hand. So surfers will say his chain is cursed, but who will find it ... ?

Matty Lowe (13)
Ashlawn School

Siege Of Carthage

War! It's all war! Everywhere I go, if it is in the area of Namidia, it's war, wherever, whenever. I am Hannibal, the leader of the Carthaginians, well I was until it fell into the hands of those Scipii Romans. Carthage gone!

My army marched across the sandy and hot coastlines setting out to conquer Egypt until one of my scouts saw them - red sails with the mark of the Scipii on them. We thought they would not come near our borders for they had taken our outpost city of Libyaeum.

I called a retreat to our city, Carthage as the Romans grew ever closer to the shores. My men were tired as they ran into our city with its high walls and golden coloured buildings. I knew that the Romans had taken the shore, for smoke had risen from where the camps would be set.

As the sun rose the next day my men gathered at the top of the wall awaiting the enemy at the city gates. Soon, one flaming arrow flew into the sky as I heard a large amount of steps getting louder and louder. It was the Scipii.

Tall siege weapons followed behind their troops. Ladders, catapults, ballistas, all weaponry. Was this all for this one batter, for this great city? I thought to myself, *so it begins ...*

The siege lasted hours as the Romans fired boulders at our walls. They put ladders on the walls and the men climbed up them to attack my archers close-up. Soon my walls fell to the enemy, with the sound of my troops dying on the walls. Soon the city was overrun, my troops had fled, so I did as well. Our city had fallen to the enemy and when I got out, I looked back at the city. It was in flames, Carthage was gone.

Jack Pooley (12)
Ashlawn School

Mike And The Dorkataur

On a sunny evening in the middle of spring, Mike was walking to his friend's house when he suddenly realised there was a football at the side of the bridge he was walking over. He picked it up and looked at it. It was a Total 90 football, but it was very flat, he was still able to kick it. He put it down on a thin bit of grass and kicked it hard over the bridge wall. He jumped on the bridge to see it drop down.

As he watched it slowly dropping in the air, he saw a child walking down the old railway under the bridge. 'Heads,' shouted Mike. The child looked up to see a football heading straight for him. Within a split second, *bang!*. It had smacked him right on his nose, making his nose look as flat as a pancake.

Mike rushed down the slope to see a child lying unconscious on the ground. He tipped water over the child's face who soon woke up and said, 'What did you think you were doing? That was a very dangerous thing you just did, I might have to report you.'

'But I only kicked a ball,' replied Mike.

The child looked angry, he got out his PSHE book as in it it showed him what to do when he got angry, hurt or annoyed, like he was now. His teacher had told him to just walk away from situations like these, but he couldn't - he was getting hot. He stood up, went face to face with Mike. Mike ran and the child ran after him.

Josh Slater (13)
Ashlawn School

Gladiator

One cold, breezy morning the battle was about to begin. The army of Spartacus was challenged by the greedy army of Achilles. Thousands started to charge, but Spartacus led his army to victory.

That night the celebrations began, but as Spartacus was going to his tent alone, survivors kidnapped him. Before any of his army had enough time to save him, he was sold the next day to be a gladiator and fight in stadiums. 'Now you will risk your life every day and we will watch you in every battle for revenge of Achilles!' They were the last words from an Achilles soldier to Spartacus before he was sold.

The first day he was scared and nervous, but he had his sword, pride and men to fight for. One after another he killed immediately and saw the faces of Achilles' men in the stadium. Day after day, he fought for people's enjoyment, moving high up into the ranks.

He wanted to earn his freedom, but the only way to do that was by winning. The crowd's choice if you stay alive in the big battle of Rome.

It came to that day and there were only eight gladiators alive versus twenty of the king's guards. However, Spartacus fought like he never had before. He was the only man still standing and shouted to everyone, 'Are you not entertained?'

The king ordered him to be executed right then for what he'd said. The crowd began to boo, but right before he was killed, his army ran on and rescued him. 'Spartacus, Spartacus, Spartacus,' the crowd roared. The king had no choice but to grant Spartacus his freedom and let his army go. He had won the crowd!

After that he was known as 'The Gladiator' and he and his army went down in history ...

Alex Shilton (13)
Ashlawn School

Tommy And The Teachertor

One fine sunny day, Tommy woke up and he jumped out of bed, shouting, 'Yeah, it's the last day of school!' He got dressed and went downstairs. Then he had some breakfast and went to school. At school, he looked up and his knees trembled with fear. At least it was the last day, but it was one he would never forget.

He walked in through the humongous gates that seemed to glare at everyone who walked through them. He met his friends, but something was not right about them - as he walked over to them, he walked straight through them. They were holograms. Tommy thought to himself, *that's weird - no one's here but holograms.*

He carried on and got to the school. No one was there. Suddenly the door slammed shut and Tommy couldn't open it.

Tommy heard a noise - he ran forward and looked around the corner. There was something there. Then all of a sudden, a figure started to run at him. It was his head teacher with horns and four legs. Tommy ran and finally got to the gym and locked himself in.

He knew that he wouldn't last long in the gym because the teachertor was already breaking down the door. Tommy ran and he saw some stairs - he ran up them and he came onto the roof. The teachertor followed. Tommy was panting, the teachertor ran at him and Tommy moved out of the way. The teachertor screamed and died on the floor. Tommy looked over and the teachertor was gone …

Tom Bennett (13)
Ashlawn School

A Day In The Life Of ...

I was running to the clearing as a blinding white light passed over my head. I ducked low as someone passed by near the fence. Something ran across the grass, coming in my direction. I saw a small bunker ahead of me, it resembled an abandoned bomb shelter but I knew there was more to it, it was also my escape and entry - everything depended on it. As I looked up at the dark blue night sky, I heard ragged, heavy breathing behind me, coming closer.

I knew there wasn't much time. I made a break for the bunker. On arrival, fear gripped me as I found it locked. I didn't belong here, this wasn't my life. I shouldn't be doing this and now it seemed that the game was up and I was finished, but then I saw him. Quickly ducking behind the sandbags and crates, I peered between a gap in the bags. I saw a lab assistant, dressed in a long, flowing, white coat, reach out to the right of the door as a concealed computer screen with a combination lock appeared. I saw him punch the numbers in, using my watch to reflect what was on the screen as I wrote it down on my arm. He was about to go in when he saw light reflecting from my watch. He withdrew a gun and came near my hiding place. I quickly sent the crates and sandbags flying at him as I rammed him in the chest, making him drop the gun and instantly collapse on the spot, unconscious. I took his coat and entered the bunker. The room was pitch-black, so I switched on the light to see what looked like a missile and some staring scientists. Something whizzed over my head as the guards came in, firing at me - so much for my disguise. I ran as fast as I could to where a conveyor belt was and dived headfirst into it. As I went through, I came to an empty corridor, which seemed endless. I ran to the only other door in the corridor. Somebody was coming behind me. I took the chance, I went into a large office. A man in a chair with his back to me was surrounded by four guards. The man spoke, 'It looks like the game is up for you, my young spy.'

Malcolm Remedios (13)
Ashlawn School

A Day In The Life Of Mother

She's moaning again and now she's got that tone. 'Wait, I'm watching my programme,' I call down demanding another ten minutes. It doesn't work. She marches me downstairs to sit at the desk, under supervision! My homework finished, still with an attitude, I go straight to bed. God, I feel strange, so tired, so tired, *zzzz*.

Ring! Ring! It's the alarm clock … what alarm clock? I glance around, one eye still asleep. 5.30am, what? I'm getting out of bed when I hear a familiar voice. It's Gran.

She bursts in angrily, grabs my ear and pulls me downstairs. 'I've been shouting you for 30 minutes,' she screams. 'Chores now, go and feed those animals.' She opens the back door and boots me outside.

I'm in the dirt, dazed and confused. Just then a young lad runs over. 'Get a move on Shelley, or you're in for a bashing!' he says. *Oh my God - he called me Shelley.* That's not me. That's Mum and he looks just like Uncle Sam!

'Sam, what year is it?' I ask cautiously.

'You big dollop!' he replies. 'It's 1976 of course,' and runs off.

I don't know how, but I am Mum. Maybe because I was so horrible. Perhaps it is punishment, God knows I deserve it. I don't want to be Mum, her childhood was nasty.

That night in bed, exhausted, feeling guilty and sorry for myself, I pray to God to let me be me again. 'I've learned my lesson,' I cry.

But now it's morning, dare I open my eyes?

Gemma Tailby (11)
Ashlawn School

A Day In The Life Of A Dog

Woof! Argh, the most famous word by a dog. Us famous mammals, a man's best friend ... well at least, most of us are. Lucky for me I am one of them, I have a loving, caring family. I have a brother called Carl, a dad called Tony and a mother called Tricia and my name's Ben.

You see my whole family are loving and caring, but when I do something wrong - say ... jump on the settee when no one's looking and the cover isn't on - they always seem to have an argument. My mum always tells me to get off or else she will smack my bottom. On the other hand, my dad will just tell me to get off so he can put the cover on and then he will let me go back on.

When it's the morning or the evening, I always get fed. If it's my mother feeding me, I get half a bowl, if it's my dad, I get a full bowl. My life is just so boring you see, most of the day and night I just sit in my cosy blue bed and go to sleep or just lie there. Occasionally my dad will take me on walks and play football, frisbee or even 100 metre sprint with me. He normally wins the football, but I beat him on the 100 metre sprint.

So really there isn't much to say about my life, except that it's boring and that a man is a dog's best friend!

Carl Mosteckyj (13)
Ashlawn School

The Ice Cream Van

Once upon a time, there was a man that wanted a job, so he went to the shop. On his way, he saw an ice cream van and on the side it said, 'Staff Wanted - £14 an hour'. He said to himself, 'That will do me!'

He had never driven before and was a very fast driver. He didn't do his round, he just carried on with the music going and him shouting, 'Run, run as fast as you can, you can't catch me, I'm the ice cream man.'

His boss asked him why he hadn't sold any ice cream and he said he hadn't stopped because energy was better than ice cream. His boss wasn't interested, he just shouted at him saying, 'Yes, it probably is, but I get more money for ice cream. Now go - you're fired!'

Joe Boyer (12)
Ashlawn School

When Aliens Attack

In a galaxy that can't be seen but does exist, a ship was under heavy fire by asteroids and other wandering ships. An alliance was formed between these ships and the aliens - they were on a killing spree to destroy and take over the galaxy. But this gun-shaped ship was not about to give up their galaxy to some heavy-weaponed aliens.

On board this ship, a warrior with extreme skills was getting prepared for battle. As he arose, the aliens had started to board through the escape pods. He was told to kill as many aliens as possible and take any remaining escape pods off the ship to safe land.

He was equipped with a shotgun and a machine gun. He went out of the room and immediately he was involved. *Bang!* He hit an alien on the head and it fell flat onto the floor. As he went through doors and killed aliens, all the escape pods had already been used by aliens to enter the ship.

He realised he was heading for the control room where the surviving humans were. He entered the room, an incoming bullet rattled the wall behind him and then they knew it was a human when he fired back a shotgun bullet.

As he approached the main control area, a voice came out of nowhere - it was the voice of the ship. She said the only way to destroy the aliens was to blow up the ship and along with it, the entire alien destroyers.

'I'm setting the ship to go off in five minutes so get the one remaining escape pod ...'

David Sargeant (12)
Ashlawn School

Zeus Has A New Job!

A few years ago at Ashlawn School, Mr Taylor had to retire because of old age. The flyers went up on all the walls, saying, *English Teacher Needed*. Zeus looked, it sounded so interesting. It also said, *Interviews Tomorrow*.

He was so excited, he got all dressed up and went to Ashlawn School. When he got there, all the children were staring at him, since he was so big and tall he could barely fit through the doors.

When he was being interviewed, they were so impressed by his presentation, they gave him the job straight away.

The next day, he went to the English room and sat at his desk. Then, *bang!* The door slammed open and the children charged in and sat at their desks. Halfway through the lesson a child wouldn't stop talking, so Zeus said, 'Die, you evil child.' He then sliced his head off, but the child just popped up again, but with six more heads and bodies. Soon there were over 1,000 pupils in the classroom.

Zeus then jumped out of the classroom and to Mr Rospter's office. Mr Rospter was very disappointed with him, and very angry. He said, 'En garde', and started sword fighting in his office. *Slice! Chop!* went Zeus and he killed Mr Rospter.

The class went, 'Noooo,' and stood there next to Mr Rospter. Then Mr Taylor came back, grabbed his sword out of nowhere and killed Zeus and everyone was very happy.

Danielle Cash (12)
Ashlawn School

A Day In The Life Of A Clay Pigeon

Dear Diary,

Well, it's my birthday today and I'm hoping and praying that I'm not fired because I will be shot by those awful men. I wanted a lovely big cake, but no such luck. I'm all alone now, poor old Benny was fired yesterday. I've no one to talk to apart from you, Diary. I miss you so much Benny.

Oh well, life must go on mustn't it? Oh dear, here comes John to select 70 of us to go through the cannon. I'll tell you more later.

Later

Yes, I'm still here. Thank you! I'm so glad. Though you may not know, Diary, they will come to get more soon. Let's not put the dampeners on things though. Well, my birthday has gone quite well, considering. I feel as if I'm being looked after. You know, I was expecting to be fired and shot, but I'm here. I must go, Tom wants more pigeons.

Later still

I'm back again! I swear someone's watching over me today! Twice they've walked past me, *twice!* I'm so happy I could burst! I'm so lucky! Tim - the clay pigeon against all odds! Oh no, he's seen me writing. Now I'm for it!

Unfortunately we never heard the rest of Tim's story. We must assume that he has now passed on.

Amy Lowe (12)
Ashlawn School

A Day In The Life Of A Fly

Monday 16th May

You know what? Being fly is tough. You have to know your neighbourhood, you have to know which houses leave the best crumbs around and, of course, you have to know the swatters. The swatters are evil humans who know where we hang out. Do you know over 500 of us flies are swatted a week!

Last week, we suffered the death of young Bob the fly. He was sitting on the top of a table peacefully eating a bit of Mars bar when *swoosh*, down came a rolled-up newspaper right on top of him. We will never forget Bob.

Tuesday 17th May

You know what? Sometimes I think that those humans think that we are s-t-u-p-i-d. I was flying around house 36 when I spotted fly tape hanging from the ceiling. *Now*, I thought, *just before Bob died, he told me about the fly tape.* I had heard of it before but never seen it. So, anyway, I managed to avoid the fly tape and head back home.

When I got home, fly Sarah and fly James came and told me that fly Tom had got himself stuck on the fly tape. Now I have never really liked Tom so I decided not to help him. Instead I sat and had a chocolate bar. Life's tough!

Stephanie Lopez (12)
Ashlawn School

Hooded Tops Sorted Out By The Cops

It has been on the telly a lot recently about youths in gangs. Some people say that it is intimidating that they are wearing 'hoodies' or 'hooded tops'. People claim this is because the children's faces can't be seen. Many people believe that everyone wearing them is up to mischief.

Shopkeepers have told us that things have been stolen from their shops but they can't find out who the culprit is.

I interviewed a child wearing one of the tops and he said, 'I haven't got a clue why people keeping moaning. Why can't we just wear what we want? It's a joke!'

I also interviewed a lady with the totally opposite point of view: 'The children don't understand the intimidation they are causing. It will do them no harm just to take the hoods off'.

A thing called 'happy slapping' is another disgraceful thing on our streets. It is when young gangs attack random people on the streets. The horrible thing about it is that they record it all on their camera phones. I'm sure that the person being slapped isn't very happy.

In my opinion, both people are right in what they are saying, but if I had to choose, I would side with the lady.

Thomas Protheroe (12)
Ashlawn School

A Day In The Life Of An Ambulance Officer

One normal day for Jeremy Rodgers had suddenly turned for the worse. He got ill, so a replacement was made. Jeremy Rodgers was replaced with 'Happy Man' (his nickname). Happy Man was very good at his job. Also he really enjoyed being there when times were rough as he could cheer everybody up.

He started his shift as normal - 12pm-6am. Happy Man and his partner got in their ambulance and drove into the city to get to a waiting point.

When they were a couple of miles from base, the red phone rang back at the station. It made the whole station rumble. It was picked up by the station officer. The call was relayed by fax to Happy Man and his partner in their ambulance.

All of a sudden, Happy Man turned into 'Driver Man'. He was extremely good at driving quickly and safely. They got to the scene within 3 minutes of the call. As they left the scene they saw something no one in their patch had seen before. A car-jacking in progress! They followed the car and the woman was thrown out. Happy Man's partner got out with a crash kit to help the lady. She had a gunshot wound. The partner told this to Happy Man who turned into 'Gunboy Mad Man', which meant he was skilled at shooting.

Suddenly he flicked a button. The red button that said *For Emergencies Only*. He pressed it and opened the gun cabinet. He got out a rifle and continued in pursuit of the car. He saw the man and fired. The man died. Happy Man was a hero.

Kallum Bell (12)
Ashlawn School

Hercules And The Loch Ness Monster

One foggy winter's day, in a village in Scotland, a local villager called Scott saw a big snake-like monster body, semi-submerged in water. He ran and ran to the nearest church and prayed. He prayed for hours until he got an answer.

Later on, a light shone from the sky, slowly and slowly it lowered until it touched the almost dry soil. Everybody took a step back except the new priest - he knew God had sent this light. The light slowly dimmed enough so that they could see a shape of a muscly man.

Then he spoke. 'Who is the person who called me down from Heaven?'

'It was me.'

'Why?'

'So you could take care of that foul beast.'

'Take me to this beast!'

The villager and the priest accompanied him to the loch. When they reached it there was no sign of this monster, but then its body emerged above the water and it looked at Hercules as if to say 'go back'. The beast submerged itself back underwater. Then Hercules jumped in after it. He could see the beast, but only just in the murky water. He swam on, then he heard a slap of a fin, and another. Then he swung his arm but missed. He swung again - he got it. It felt quite light, no weight at all. He pulled it out to see - it wasn't the beast! He then got hit on the head and was never seen again. The monster stayed alive!

Aaron Batten (12)
Ashlawn School

A Day In The Life Of ...

Dear Diary,

I'm a parent now, but my adopted kids don't know that I'm an alien and my husband is too.

Today is Christmas Eve and 3 children keep on going on about presents. What are presents? Lucy wants some telescopey thing and Gabbie wants some music-listening thing. I've seen and listened to her old one - I think it's cool. I don't know what TJ wants. Oh no, I'm a bad mother! I don't know what he wants!

It doesn't matter! They already think we're weird. I put dog baskets out for their beds. How am I supposed to know they want human beds? They're always complaining. I made mashed potato with frogspawn in it. I got the frogspawn from the big hole in the ground. For dessert I made cooked rats - I found those in the basement. I thought they'd love it, especially when they're fresh.

Lucy goes on about this man called 'Father Christmas'. She goes on like he's so special. Gabbie told me he's not real. Why would people be so mean and tell her he's real? Tomorrow they're going to be so upset. I know - I'll make them a nice Christmas dinner. That will cheer them up, won't it? I can't think of anything else to do. I only started this diary because Lucy told me about it. I got well excited! I'm so stuck, what should I do? Will I cope? I have to tell them our little secret.

Heera Govind (12)
Ashlawn School

A Day In The Life Of My Super Hero

My super hero is the busiest, most fantastic person in the world! My super hero is Rainbow, she is the most brilliant super hero ever born! And today I'm going to be her!

'Oh my gosh,' I yelped, looking at the clock. 'I'm late, I'm late!'

I rushed to the wardrobe and put on my most fantastic suit, my rainbow outfit. I looked at my astro-watch and decided there was no time for breakfast. I ran like lightning down the road and took off into the sky.

Flying is probably the best feeling in the world. I flew with speed to the gym. I had just got on the running machine when my watch began bleeping. I was needed in the city centre. I was off in a flash.

Stood on top of a skyscraper, I looked down into a small side alley to see a circle of youngsters surrounding a single child. I flew down and they all spread apart. The little one was crying so I gave him a hug. I turned around to see the bullies trying to creep off. I stretched out my super-length arms and pulled them back. I made them say sorry and told them I'd be watching. As for the little one, I flew him home.

That was just a typical day and now I'm off for some popcorn at the cinema with my boyfriend, Lightning Bolt.

Megan Harding (12)
Ashlawn School

Cats, Cats Everywhere (But Not For Long)

It was Friday 13th August when a milk truck was included in an accident with a really big truck. The truck swerved into the milk truck at very high speed and made a big hole in the side of it. Milk was pouring everywhere.

As the milk poured, so did the amount of cats.

An investigator interviewed Lucy Stent who was a driver close by at the same time as it happened.

She said, 'Well, I wasn't looking when it crashed, but I saw the milk pour everywhere and suddenly loads of cats came flooding in.'

Later on, the investigator found out something about the milk, something very, very bad and disgusting …

Kirsty Montgomery (12) & Samantha Peel (11)
Ashlawn School

A Day In The Life Of A Victorian Pupil

Dear Diary,

Today was the worst day of my life. It started off as a normal day. I was woken brutally by Mother yelling at me to get up and do my chores, but then my little sister ate my breakfast and Mother said it was my fault because I didn't get up quickly enough.

I did all the chores and ran to school. I was late. An evil grin spread over Mr Pointing's face when I arrived at school just ten minutes after the bell - that earned 3 hits with the cane. We did my worst subject, maths. I was falling behind, so guess what happened - one more hit. After maths we did English - my best and favourite subject. We did spelling - it was long and uneventful. When we finally finished, he told us to write a 1,000 word essay on spelling rules. I said, 'But Sir ...' that was my mistake of the day. That earned me 4 hits. I'd broken my record. Just at that moment I heard a small ring and I, along with everyone else, ran home.

When I eventually got home, I was sent out to the farm to help Father plough the field.

It's now 12.30 - very late. My family went to bed at 8.30 and that's considered late. I've finished my essay and I'm falling asleep.

Goodnight.

Jessica Perkins (12)
Ashlawn School

The Twisted Story Of Robin Hood

In a land far, far away, there was a woodland and the rich people lived there. There also lived the poor people who lived in huts. They were poor and didn't live very well.

It all started on a lovely, hot, beautiful day when the poor people were planning to take over and kill their landlord. They called him 'The Master of Destruction'.

The next day they went to take the Master of Destruction. They were singing, 'Hi-ho, hi-ho, it's time for the rich people to go, oh, oh. Hi-ho, hi-ho, hi-ho!'

They arrived at the rich forest and first they sneaked in and stole money, clothes and good, expensive belongings. Then they got a fire lamp (a big stick of wood) with a flame on the top and started to set everything on fire. The poor were happy and now rich.

So the poor turned to rich and the rich turned to poor and they lived a happy life - nearly anyway. They mostly lived happily ever after.

Alice Wong (12)
Ashlawn School

The Curse Of Tutankhamen

Carter stood at what he thought was the tomb of a young Egyptian pharaoh. Standing at this sealed door he pierced a hole in the top left-hand corner.

'Can you see anything?' asked Lord Carnarvon, who had joined him on this expedition.

'Oh yes,' replied Carter. 'Wonderful things.'

It was the autumn of 1922. In the tomb there was an old rag lying on the floor - it was probably from grave robbers over 3,000 years ago.

Little did they know that they had unleashed a 3,000-year-old curse that would follow them to the grave.

It all started when Lord Carnarvon died of a mosquito bite just 7 weeks after the expedition. When they examined Tutankhamen they found the same bite on him and on his left-hand cheek! Exactly where Lord Carnarvon's was!

Loads of people died from this curse, then out of the blue an American with the surname 'Carter' died.

As if that wasn't enough, a few years later a bystander, who was at the opening, threw a vase at a wall in his flat. He wrote a note which stated, 'I can't stand any more horrors'. He then jumped out of his lounge window. When police examined the vase they found that it was a vase from Tutankhamen's tomb! His brother also committed suicide. He was named the twenty-first victim.

Then a Paris museum keeper got given some of Tutankhamen's possessions. He got hit by a truck the following day.

Is the curse true? Nobody knows.

Georgia May (11)
Ashlawn School

Who Do You Back?

Both Manchester United and Chelsea Football Clubs are battling for the biggest prize in club football. To be crowned the kings of Europe by winning the UEFA Champions League at the Millennium Stadium in Cardiff.

Chelsea

What can I say about this club … ? They have been the success story of the season under new ownership by Russian billionaire, Roman Abramovich, and a new manager, José Mourinho. They have turned this London club around.

Man Utd

The Red Devils have a reputation in European football that they are a team to be reckoned with. Managed by the faithful Alex Ferguson and owned by the hated Malcolm Glazer, United's good youth development will show as they play a slightly younger, less experienced side.

Pre-Match Analysis

I believe that the big battle tonight will be in the central midfield as both teams have fresh, young frontmen to bang them in. Therefore, it will be the service coming in from the midfield from Keane and Maketele that will make a difference tonight. Match prediction - I reckon Chelsea will just about clinch this one with their multimillion pound, young, fresh, skilful side!

Nick Brown (13)
Ashlawn School

They Turn It Off After 15 Years

Today, the owner of St Cross Hospital in Rugby finally convinced the parents of Mrs Connifer to let their daughter be put to rest after 15 years of her being on a life support machine. Mr Downer (the owner of the hospital) has had hundreds of meetings with the Connifers but they were not convinced that she was gone. The mother, Patricia, said, 'I love her so much and I wouldn't be able to live with myself if I knew I was the one who ended our and her hopes of survival. But 15 years after her near-fatal accident we had lost all faith'.

The parents used to sit in the hospital day after day, even though their daughter was brain-dead.

Mr Downer has said about today's news, 'We had no choice but to ask them to let their loved one go to Heaven and rest, as we have had to refrain from putting people on wards as there was not a spare bed. We are very sorry but thankful to the Connifers for the decision they decided to make after one and a half decades of waiting'.

The machine was turned off at 3.23am and the hospital seems to have a very cold atmosphere since the plug was pulled. The family of the girl left at 4.30am after thanking all the doctors, nurses and other staff for the support they have given to their lifelong wounded household.

A very sad day for the Connifers but a special one too.

Jake Batchelor (13)
Ashlawn School

Happy Slaps Don't Get Claps!

Recently the demand among young children and teenagers for video phones is rising due to the new craze of 'happy slapping'. This is where children go around slapping random people and videoing it on their phones. This is a worry for many people as it has started happening outside the schools.

The news of the extreme measures some teenagers are taking comes after the recent ban in some shopping centres of hooded tops. This is because older people feel intimidated because of the big gangs and because the hoods conceal their identity.

The gangs of youths are now taking this playground craze to the streets and attacking members of the public. The craze of 'happy slapping' has gone from one extreme to the other. It started off as something in the playground and has now turned into random attacks in the streets and on buses.

One victim of this was Peter Green, who was set on fire as he slept in a bus stop after a night out, and his terrible ordeal was all captured on camera.

This craze has now reached its limits and it is time it is stopped before someone is killed. Many schools have banned phones and shops won't sell video phones to anyone under 18 years old. This should be stopped now.

Daniel Haynes (12)
Ashlawn School

A Day In The Life Of A Boy Called Timmy

Straightening his blue wavy hair, Timmy strolled lazily along the path heading for John's house, his best friend. His bright blue trainers stood out in the hot, dry afternoon. He was not expecting an afternoon and night of danger.

Timmy walked up to the big brown door and knocked twice, then waited patiently. He heard John's heavy footsteps coming nearer to the door ...

'Hi Timmy,' said John. 'Please come in.' John's light green eyes were flashing, waiting for an answer, and his bright red hair was in the same wavy design as Timmy's.

Timmy stepped inside the warm house and joyfully followed his friend to his room. *The room is wonderful*, thought Timmy, staring around. His bedroom was the size of half a football pitch and the decoration was of the football team he supported, Liverpool.

There was a loud *bang!* Timmy got frightened and looked back. He was confused. John had closed and locked his door.

'Why ... ?' began Timmy, but suddenly he was facing an animal which was fierce as a lion, scary as an elephant. It was a huge poisonous snake. Timmy had no time to think, he began running around the huge bedroom, terrified, with the green devil hissing at his feet.

I need a weapon, thought Timmy quickly. As though he'd brought it, he found a sharp, small, black sword lying on the floor. Did he dare to take it? Without thinking, he picked up the weapon and threw it fiercely on the creature.

'Argh!'

Omar Elbayouk (12)
Ashlawn School

Giant Hamster On The Loose

In the early hours of Friday morning, there had been several sightings of a 'giant hamster'. We went to investigate the reports and to our surprise we found that the sightings were real.

We investigated where the giant hamster had come from. A spokesman for Animal Testing Inc admitted that the hamster, named Tiny, had escaped from their local lab.

He explained that Tiny was a failed experiment and stressed that the public were in no danger, but he warned people not to approach Tiny in case they scared him and got trampled and sat on. He also admitted that Tiny was no longer required and that if no home was found then he would have to be shot dead.

Local Zoo Saves Hamster

Local zoologist, Zoe Zoomaker, has come to Tiny's rescue by volunteering to take him in. After an 8-hour operation, Tiny was safely captured and is now happily living in the local zoo.

Sophie Rawlings (12)
Ashlawn School

Hercules Vs Ashlawn

As everyone knows, Hercules is a strong man. But one day he was bored so he decided to come to Ashlawn School.

It was a Monday morning and Year 7 were in their usual boring English class with Mr Taylor.

'Right everyone, what is a simile?'

'I know,' shouted Hassina.

'I'm going to ask Gemma,' said Mr Taylor.

But just as Gemma was about to answer, there was a knock at the door.

'Mr Taylor,' said a voice.

The door opened and in came Hercules.

'Wow!' everyone gasped.

'It's my fave hero!' shouted Ryan.

'I'm going to take this class today,' said Hercules.

'Right, I'll get my coat then.'

A few minutes later, Hercules started to speak. 'Right,' he shouted. 'I don't want any shouting. No messing around and no throwing,' he yelled.

Everyone was silent until someone started to speak - it was Bobby. He never listened to anyone. Then everyone else started to speak. They carried on until Hercules went mad. He pulled out his knife and chopped Bobby's head in half.

'Argh!' screamed Steph.

But then not only did Bobby recover - there grew 3 more of him. Everyone was still shouting so then Hercules cut everyone's head off, but then everyone tripled.

'Get him!' yelled Steph.

'Yeah, come on!' screamed Hassina.

'Argh! Help!'

Then Charlie started kicking him and Megan started punching him.

'That's it!' he yelled. 'I'm never coming back.'

Mr Taylor came in. 'Did you have fun?' he asked.

Hassina Shabbir (12)
Ashlawn School

A Day In The Life Of A Soldier

'Hi Tom, do you see anything?' Ally asked.

'No. You?' Tom replied to him.

'No, hang on a minute,' Ally said very quietly. 'There is something out there,' Ally said, scared.

'What is it?'

Then all of a sudden, Ally jumped down out of the trees and woke everyone up, ready for battle. Ally was alongside Tom all the way, they would always look out for each other.

It was quiet for 10 minutes - all you could hear were the birds singing along to each other. Then one of the German troops fired and gave away their position. Ally and Tom were commanded by their stupid general to go round the side and risk their lives for England.

Then, out of the distance, came around 100 German troops. They were walking straight for Ally and Tom. The birds' beautiful singing was blocked out by the sound of gunfire. The Germans could only see Ally and Tom, so the English waited for them to get closer and closer.

It took about 5 minutes for them to get into full range. Then *boom!* One of the English threw a grenade at the Germans. They turned around and started to run back. Tom jumped out of his ditch and chased after them, but it was a trick. Tom got shot right through his head.

All of the English jumped out and started to shoot. Ally charged right for the guy that had shot Tom, to kill him. On the way, Ally got shot in the arm and then the leg. Ally fell to the ground in pain, but then climbed back up and was shot in the leg again. One of his men came and carried him back to the hospital ward.

Karl Fisher (12)
Ashlawn School

Disaster Strikes!

Hundreds of rescue teams were called out last night after a huge disaster.

In the small town of Rugby, a huge flood took place; rushing waters took away everything in sight, hundreds of homes were destroyed and people had nowhere to go.

People's homes were left swept out, no furniture, nothing, just the strong stench of sewage and mud. Many people had to be evacuated from their homes after having no flood warning at all.

After everyone was safe in a town nearby, Rugby Borough Council had to figure out a way of pumping the sewage-filled water out of Rugby.

Eventually they did; huge pumps were put in the murky water to clear the town's floor. After a couple of hours, the town was clear but houses were left destroyed. Farmland, shops, everything was ruined.

All the water was put in a reservoir nearby but nothing will fix the way thousands of people watched their homes float away.

Townspeople will try and help build a new Rugby.

Fabulous new shops are to be built and hopefully the town will become a brand new, shining place for many people to live.

Ella Slatcher (11)
Ashlawn School

A Day In The Life (And Death) Of Sniff

Sniff was a cat, a rather stupid cat, a rather skinny cat and, unfortunately for him, a very curious cat. To some, the name 'Sniff' might sound like a dog's name, but he doesn't do 'cat things'. For example, he doesn't bury his poo, he doesn't play with string and he also doesn't clean himself, evidently making him a rather smelly cat as well. Neither does he try to catch mice or birds, because being a stupid cat, the mice and birds notice him before he notices them. Sniff doesn't have a home, well, not anymore. His curiosity led him so far away from his house that when he decided to turn back, he had no idea where he was. As he had no one to feed him, his diet consisted mainly of mouldy garbage.

One day, as Sniff was finishing off his mouldy milk and chicken scraps breakfast, he noticed a fresh chunk of cheese beside the bin he was eating out of. He dived at it head-first. Even as the huge metal bar closed in on top of his head, he didn't realise that it was a big rat trap.

Sniff woke up on a cloudy bed and realised he was in Heaven, but it didn't take him long to realise he was in a horrible place! Poo had to be buried, there was string as far as the eye could see and washing yourself was a daily routine! He jumped back down to cat hell and realised that he liked it a lot better down there.

James McCallum (13)
Ashlawn School

A Day In The Life Of John Jo

Operation: No School

'*Wake up,* John Jo! I've been calling you for half an hour now. If you don't get out of bed, you're gonna be late for school.'

John Jo opened his eyes. *Oh no, not another schoolday,* he thought. He slowly got out of bed. As he was getting dressed he noticed his calendar. Tuesday 6th October. That date seemed to remind him of something.

Later on, he was walking to school when he remembered what he was meant to be doing on that day. He quickly ran off in the opposite direction. As he skidded into the car park he noticed a gang of boys. He walked over to them.

'You remembered, John Jo,' shouted one of the boys.

'Yeah, I remembered, just in time. But believe me, I wouldn't miss it for the world,' he replied. 'OK then, let's start operation, *no school.*'

It was half-past two and the day was nearly over. John Jo was sort of glad because it was starting to get tiring. Nothing had happened so far. The most entertaining thing was probably when the gang leader had turned around and accidentally walked head-first into a wall. It didn't take a genius to tell that he shouldn't have bothered coming.

It was half-past three and time to go. As John Jo started walking home he heard a scream. He ran back to where it had come from and he found his best mate, Benedict, lying dead on the floor. '*Noooo!*' he screamed. 'Whoever did this is going to *paaaaay!*'

Ollie Vale (13)
Ashlawn School

Dragon Danger

Recently, a dragon has been spotted in the local area. Here is Fiona Barr with the story.

'Yes, I am here in Coventry where all the action is happening. It started last night when unfortunately the dragon opened his eyes. Fortunately, the prince was invisible at the time and couldn't be seen. Suddenly he'd heard a cry from aloft. The almighty dragon had got up and was patrolling the area like a submarine in defence. The prince flew up high. It was nearly impossible for the dragon to see him.

The dragon didn't give up. Swooping around his chosen building, he came down and deactivated his wings whilst lying on the road. The prince's cloak was torn and made him visible again. The dragon flew back up into the sky, right to the prince's position. The prince submerged himself into nearby bushes for cover. The dragon flew straight past, looked around and went off into the distance. Without waiting any longer, the prince went to save the screaming princess.

Well, that was the scene here yesterday, but now I think the prince and princess have plans to get married, so here it's all round happiness.'

Daniel Evans (13)
Ashlawn School

William The Conqueror Takes Over England
Harold Killed By Arrow!

King Edward had died and Harold took over as king. William, the Duke of Normandy, was very angry because King Edward had said that he would become King of England.

William told his Norman soldiers to go to England by boat to fight a battle. The Norman soldiers had to row across the English Channel. It was hard work.

Meanwhile, Harold of England was fighting a battle with his soldiers in the North of England. The English soldiers were very tired.

William landed near Hastings, so Harold had to march his soldiers to Hastings. Harold's men were exhausted. William and Harold set up camps. The soldiers had to carry all of their equipment.

The Norman and English soldiers had a nasty battle. Lots of soldiers died, killed by bows and arrows, swords and spears. The conditions were very bad.

Harold was killed by an arrow through his eye. William took the crown of England. He is now known as William the Conqueror.

Class S1 (11-12)
Brooke School

Hitman Vs Shooter

As I woke up at 8 o'clock, I slowly moved out of my bed. I looked in the mirror and mumbled, 'This is the day I get revenge.'

My dad got killed when I turned 19 by a gang member and this is my day to get revenge! The gang member is called David Mitchell, nickname 'Shooter'. That man ruined my life. Now he will suffer like I did.

Oh, my name is Bradley, nickname 'Hitman'. I used to be in the same gang as Shooter but I left when I found out he set up my dad to get killed. I could see now the rumours going round the streets; *Hitman Vs Shooter*, but he is a very dangerous man, so I'm going to work alone.

I used to be a very successful footballer, I played for Liverpool and England until my dad died. I can still see him lying on the floor, bleeding and screaming. That day was the worst day of my life.

Shooter will be dead tonight.

It's now 7 o'clock and I'm in an alleyway waiting for him. I see him. He stares at me. I look at him and in one blink I pull the trigger. He is on the floor looking exactly how my dad did. Now I've got my revenge and there's nothing to live for. I've left a letter on my bed, I just hope my mum understands.

Darren Jackson (14)
Coundon Court School & Community College

Gunners' 'Spot' Of Luck

Lehmann The Hero As Arsenal Triumph In Penalty Shoot-Out.

Jens Lehmann, the Arsenal goalie, fulfilled his dreams yesterday as he saved a penalty from Paul Scholes of the opposite team. Lehmann's spot kick save capped an outstanding individual performance, which helped the Gunners Cardiff.

Despite being out-played throughout the day by Man Utd, overall it was a remarkable turn around in fortunes for the German keeper who, 5 months ago, was an Arsenal 'let-down'.

After countless errors and mistakes, manager, Arsenal Wenger was on the lookout for a new keeper in the summer transfer market. Before yesterday Jen's future at Highbury looked incredibly in doubt!

A combination of heroics from Lehmann and poor finishing from Man Utd meant that United were unable to convert their superior play into goals as Arsenal came out with the final say.

Jaspreet Shoker (14)
Coundon Court School & Community College

Mystery

'Mum, I just got an email off Harry,' Charlotte said.

'You couldn't have … he's dead. I know it must be hard for you coming to terms with your brother's death but it is something you have to accept, we have to accept. Somebody must be playing a sick joke on us.'

'But it is his email address …'

'It *can't* be. Somebody must've hacked into his account,' Mum shouted.

'Who would do such a thing?'

The phone rang, 'I'll get it, Mum,' Charlotte said. 'Hello?'

'Did you get my email?'

'Email?'

'Charlotte, it's me Harry …'

She slammed the phone down.

'I'm going out, Mum,' Charlotte shouted up the stairs.

'OK, take your mobile and be back by 6pm,' Mum replied.

Charlotte needed to clear her head. It couldn't be Harry, could it? He'd been dead for two years; who would play such a sick joke? Maybe someone from school? She needed to find out the truth …

Suddenly she tripped over a log. 'Ouch!' Charlotte exclaimed.

'Here, let me help you.'

'Thanks,' Charlotte said.

'Here are your glasses; one of the lenses is cracked.'

'Great my mum is going to kill me.' She adjusted her glasses and put them back on. 'Harry?' she screamed.

'Yes, it's me, Harry,' he replied.

'But you're dead, we identified your body!' Charlotte exclaimed.

'I'm not dead, Charlotte, and I never have been,' Harry said.

'But … How … ? What … ? Why … ? So it was you who sent the email?'

'Yes,' Harry replied.

'No! It can't be. Get away from me,' Charlotte screamed as she ran away from Harry.

Rebecca Hitchings (14)
Coundon Court School & Community College

Angel Rock

(In the style of 'Angel Rock' by Darren Williams)

Not knowing what hit me. Head throbbing like a drumbeat inside my brain. There were buzzing sounds in my ears like loud music had been played. The pain was unbearable!

I lifted up, still in total agony; I took a long hard look around. I was in a dark, threatening room all on my own. I stood up slowly, not making a sound. My heart was in my throat, beating faster and faster by the second. A clash was heard from along the way, I froze still and waited … and waited!

She wiped her eyes clear of sleep and sat up in her bed. She took a look in the bed next to her. Empty. The freshly made bedspread had not been touched. She clambered out of her bed and hurried down the stairs to find the house deserted. *No trace of Mum, nor Dad, not even Liam. Where had they gone?* They wouldn't have left without telling her, they wouldn't even leave her on her own.

The place fell silent and the room was dark and mysterious. I'd never felt this scared in my life. *How is Amy? Where are Mum and Dad? What am I doing here? Who's brought me here?* All of these questions ran through my mind. *Do they know I am here?*

She reached for her rusting keys and ran out the house in a panic. She sprinted into the middle of the street in total despair. *'Liam!'* she cried, and re-called a few more times but still there was no reply!

Leanne Pitt (14)
Coundon Court School & Community College

The Swamp Creature

The swamp creature is a hideous monster, it lives in swamps but you never know which one 'cause it likes to go to different swamps. It is an ugly freak of nature; it has seven red eyes that glow like fire. At the back it has a long tail which, if it touches you, injects a deadly poison that kills you in two hours. It has four arms with sharp claws that can rip through anything. In the middle of its body it has a big mouth surrounded by seven eyes. Its mouth has four sharp teeth that stick out; for a head it has a sort of crushed shell and on top of that it has two big green horns. On its arms it has grey spikes; all over its body some of its slimy green skin is peeling off.

The swamp creature is so evil that yesterday it found some kids in the swamp.

'Wow, look at the swamp, it's bubbling,' one of the kids said.

'No, it's not,' the other kid said, but the swamp was bubbling.

Then suddenly without warning the swamp creature jumped out of the swamp.

'L-l-let's go!' the third kid said and ran.

The swamp creature roared, then ran after them. It grabbed two of them but the third kept running. The tail of the creature shot out and touched the kid who collapsed on the ground; his face turned green which meant the poison was working. The creature raised its claws then killed the kids and put their heads on sticks and walked off in search of a new swamp.

Stephen Harley (14)
Coundon Court School & Community College

Lisa Chavette's Day Out

As Lisa Chavette walked into One-Stop, the shopkeeper knew exactly what sort of character she was. With the Burberry clothes and the brown, highlighted blonde hair, a ring on each finger weighing her down, she was obviously the roughest girl in town.

When she was walking around the shop, the shopkeeper sneakily followed her just in case she robbed anything. She never bought anything though.

All Lisa did was go to the counter and say in a commanding voice, 'Give me a packet of fags!'

George Tunnicliffe (13)
Coundon Court School & Community College

The Ship

The ship's bows crashed through the waves of the blue seas. The whole ship creaked from the pressure as if it were singing. Jagged rocks stuck up out at angles surrounding an island full of stony mountains and unknown caves. The sailors of the ship were brave and loved their captain greatly with as much respect as a man could. The captain was called Usyruss of Greece and a lord just under the Emperor.

All of his men were up on deck doing their best to bail out the water and fix the mast, but all was in vain, for that storm that was brewing was far too big; so they sailed towards the islands, making their way past the rocks that could destroy the strongest ship.

Then, out of nowhere, the sound of the sea suddenly stopped and a beam of light shone upon one of the smoother-looking rocks. Three women, or what looked like women but with tails instead of legs as if they were fish, and their skin above looked as soft as silk. All their hair was fair and it blew in the wind. Suddenly, they started to sing, all three of them, a song so beautiful, so delicate and fragile that it should never have even touched a human's ears. Usyruss was transformed in a minute: carefree, happy like he was in a trance; all he wanted to do was see these maidens. But some of the more experienced sailors knew better. They grabbed him and tore him back to the mast and bound him there just as he was about to throw himself into the sea towards them. The sailors made an offering of gold to Poseidon for a safe journey and for the storm not to rise again, so they sailed northwards and the sea stayed peaceful but with a breeze to carry them.

After ten long years of sailing, Usyruss returned to Greece and became the Emperor for many years after!

Matthew Parsons (13)
Coundon Court School & Community College

Untitled

(In the style of Margaret Atwood)

I run and run, even though my legs have turned to jelly. I know I have to keep going. Twigs snap under my feet, thin branches scratch my face. I run blindly, my arms stretched forward protecting my face, my feet skimming the ground.

Was it still behind me? I could not stop to check, it would get me, get me …

My temples are pounding, my breathing, heavy and rapid.

In the distance I hear my baby scream, howl out for me. I had to leave her, I could not wait. Tears stream down my face, her cries echo in my mind. I can't leave her to that creature. I just can't.

I skid around, nearly falling over. The dry leaves kick up and the creature shrieks in anger.

I put my hand on my side as a huge pain tears through. As I raise it, blood trickles down my hand. I look down and gape in shock. A hole in my side, a hole in my side …

Something distracts me, my baby, I see her but she is fading, the pain is taking over. I lean on her and weep, stroking her head, telling her things are going to be all right. But they aren't. I stop and let the pain wash over me.

Rebecca Sweet (14)
Coundon Court School & Community College

Character Profile - Threndil

(In the style of 'Lord of the Rings' by J R R Tolkein)

Threndil, sheathing his sword, mounted his faithful horse, Thornback. He was a tall, strong, human elder, who had seen many battles. His armour, though struck by many a sword, still retained its perfect glint, the golden metal reflecting the sunlight perfectly. Inside Threndil's war helmet his face was young, carrying scars, yet the ocean-blue of his eyes illustrated his youth. He was young for an Elder, only fifty, but still held the respect of many from the upper echelons of the empire.

Although respected and trusted, this did not reflect his thoughts towards the imperial senate, which argued and fought over petty laws, while the empire was attacked from all sides. He'd often thought of appealing to General Doran, but he was a single-minded megalomaniac, who used the empire's forces for looting riches and keep them for his own devices. The senate had no power and was too full of bureaucracy to see through Doran's plots of embezzlement. The world, at least for the moment, was harsh. Threndil only trusted his horse, Thornback, who was the night-black horse, sharing lineage with horses used by emperors of old.

Threndil, galloping through the myriad of roads towards the palace was being watched. In the dark shadows was a man, silent, ghostly. He would have killed Threndil and accepted the bounty, but this was not the time or place. When the darkness of the night casts its veil, he will strike …

Tom Bromley (14)
Coundon Court School & Community College

Untitled

(In the style of 'The Princess Diaries' by Meg Cabot)

22nd November

I can't believe this. How could he? He wouldn't? I'm kidding myself. Of course Liam would be interested in girls, other than me, but ... *ahhh,* I'm so annoyed. What does Louise have that I don't? I mean she's blonde, blue-eyed, 5 feet 2, and has a style to die for, but I thought he and I were becoming really friendly. I might as well sit down in a corner and slit my throat! What happens if they get engaged or married? Okay, now I'm overreacting, they're only seeing each other. I mean it's not like they're going out.

23rd November

OMG! I'm such a freak. The last bit of street cred I had has now been flushed down the pan. I mean, anyone would have thought if a present arrived on your desk with '*Love, L*' any girl's mind would wonder if it was from Liam, the love of my life, wouldn't they? Well, I made that mistake. When I got to school there was a box on my desk, I opened it to find . . .

> 'Meet me outside the bike shed,
> *love, L'.*

I couldn't wait any longer so when Liam walked through the door with his blue sparkly eyes and blond curtains, I ran to him like I was in slow motion and pecked him on his lips. When I was just getting used to my dream moment, I was thrust to the floor, then Liam said, 'Get off me you dirty freak. I've got a girlfriend.' Then the whole class burst into laughter.

Adele Kenny (14)
Coundon Court School & Community College

Green Fingers

Wow, it's my turn. It is really my turn. They are finally coming for me and my friends, I am thinking as the shiny scrap of what I believe is a car pulls up beside me. The other shiny object, I hear people often calling it a 'chainsaw' or something, moves towards me with a strange sound similar to the one the car makes but more vicious. I have heard this many times before but I have never had the liberty of having it done to me before and now it is my turn. It tickles …

The previous scenery around me has now changed to the flashing of many other images. It is unbelievably different. It's funny how the world can change and look so different in a matter of seconds and minutes. Things I have never seen before and may never see again. It is so first time and maybe last.

A screeching noise brings to a halt the journey I have been looking forward to all my life. The big moving human pulls me from the back of the rusting car, scattered with remains of my friends and family, all dried-out and dead.

Is this the pleasure of the afterlife I am witnessing and living? Were they actually lying to me before? I wonder if I ever will get to live like the rumoured myth, like having my own field or garden.

'Help! This is not actually that fun, really.'

I am stuck to a post with a type of communication on me. It looks like my old friend. I wonder where he went. What kind of sick place is this? My friend is hanging round my neck and a man, smartly dressed, seems to look pleased.

'I want that tree please,' he says.

Jake Bevan (13)
Coundon Court School & Community College

Untitled

(In the style of 'Noughts and Crosses' by Malorie Blackman)

Tara

It was so awkward seeing him again. Seeing his big brown eyes and his ruffled brown hair just made me think back to all the happy times we spent together. I saw him at the cinema today. He was with his friends. But as soon as our eyes caught each other, I turned away. I couldn't bear to look him in the eye. Not after what he'd done.

Ben

I saw her. The only girl I ever loved, Tara. I hurt her so badly in the past. I wish I could turn back time so I didn't make that mistake again. Seeing her today just reminded me of the good times we've spent together. I have to see her again. Even if it kills me.

Tara

I dreamt about him last night. I don't know why, but ever since I saw him I can't stop thinking about him. Mother knows something is wrong.

'You're in your own little world again, Tara,' she keeps saying to me. The last time she said that to me was when Ben and I were together.

Ben

She's all I can think about. I want to be with her. If only she knew how I felt. I wish I could feel the warmth of her body and the softness of her lips against mine. I wish I could feel her long blonde hair against my skin. I wish I could see her again.

Jessica Moore (13)
Coundon Court School & Community College

Escape From Life

(In the style of Margaret Atwood)

Snout up, ears pricked and front leg raised. I heard the distant padding of paws, *run, quick!* My small brain ordered me to run, I complied with the order.

Nimbly dodging fallen branches, avoiding trees, I heard a resounding crack throughout my home, reverberating against trees, passing me like a thousand whispers of malevolence.

My muscles ceased up and I fell to the floor, anyone looking would have seen me, a three-month-old gazelle, lying weeping for my mother. My cries sped up the padding paws, the lions were getting closer, another loud cry screamed past me, closely tailed by another. These strange animals, really, *bang,* frightened me. They were fast, *bang,* loud, *bang,* and petrifying. *Bang!*

I looked down at my splayed legs, *spindly, wiry.* Where were these words coming from? *Mother.* I looked down at a red puddle gradually growing bigger around me. *Water.* I lapped at it tasting the coppery tang. *Bang!*

I gave a weak smile as I saw the heavy-breathing lions nearby, two-legged as it were. They approached, I cried, they got closer and louder. The sound of breathing made me shiver; they filled my head with memories of past times. *Bang! Bang!*

I succumbed to the darkness, the endless darkness; I heard and smelt the familiar scent of my mother. That sweet smell of gazelle fur. I had finally escaped life. I had finally escaped the pain. *Bang,* the resounding sound, *bang,* that hateful sound. *Bang! Bang!*

Abdul Almajdub (14)
Coundon Court School & Community College

Untitled

(In the style of 'The Princess Diaries' by Meg Cabot)

Thursday 5th May

She says it's going to be OK, not that I don't believe her, but how will it ever be OK again? Public humiliation is not OK, especially not in front of the entire school, not in front of my school. My school is one of those schools that makes fun of everyone who does something wrong. It's one of those schools that laugh at you even though they're laughing at something you did four years before. It's the same as every other school.

Today was the one day I was dreading. I knew I was going to make a fool of myself and I did. I was right. My mum didn't believe me, she said I was going to be fine; she said I knew what I was doing, but she was wrong. Actually very, very wrong. It's all her fault, she told me to join and I did. I'm such a fool, I should have said no.

I don't know what happened. I felt so queasy but I didn't think anything of it, because I always do before I have to present something. I was standing at the front on the stage; everyone was staring at me like I was important. And then I threw up. It was not a pretty sight. And that's not even the worst bit. I threw up on the cutest guy at school. How will I ever live this down?

OK, I've come to the conclusion that I am jinxed.

Laura Morton (14)
Coundon Court School & Community College

Eyes Of Frost

(In the style of 'Stargirl' by Jerry Spinelli)

You could tell there was a draught in the classroom by looking at her ankles, already chalk-white, the give-away was her long baby-doll dress. It was blowing around her legs, occasionally revealing fresh goose pimples. She had no shoes, her feet were bare. She dug them into the thin carpet to try and stop them trembling, it didn't work. My eyes moved up her slim body and fell at her lap, her pale, slender fingers sat there twitching nervously. She saw me. Her grey but compelling eyes blinked at me, her long eyelashes touching her pinking cheeks.

Everything about her was unusual. Even her hair, it was so blonde it was almost silver; when she shook her head the locks of hair almost sparkled. She was so frosty and wintry-looking, she appeared to belong in 'Narnia'. And even though she was quiet and strange, everyone's head was turned to her. The staring made her nervous. She blushed even more and started to pick at the threads on her pale blue shawl, draped around her shoulders. She was so delicate, like an antique.

'Now, class, today we have a new student with us ...' Miss Shorn's voice chimed. I wasn't listening. Just staring ... staring at her parted lips that I was so desperate to kiss and run my tongue along those perfect white teeth. Suddenly she stood up and walked to the front of the class. 'Everyone, this is Freya. Freya Frost.'

Freya ... my beautiful new love.

Tara Wilson (14)
Coundon Court School & Community College

Haunted

Sam tripped, twisting her ankle. Her heart stopped. She dragged herself to her feet and limped, not daring to turn.

'Samantha ...'

If she couldn't see him, he couldn't be there. He wasn't there. She winced, sensing footsteps growing closer.

'Samantha ...' He was near, malevolence clear in his footsteps. 'Samantha ... don't ignore me ...'

Sam allowed one hot tear to flow before wiping it away.

He placed his hand on her shoulder. 'Don't ignore me, Samantha ... I see straight through you...' He pulled her around.

'Leave me alone,' she begged crying.

'No, Samantha ...' He shoved her. 'I won't leave you alone ...'

Sam fell, sliding down a tree.

'Get up.'

She crawled past him, pulling herself up. He turned, pushed her against a tree.

'Samantha ...' Sam flailed. He hit her and slammed her back. He then did things she couldn't forget. When he had finished, he took out a knife and rested it against her throat. 'Tell me you love me.' Silence.

He pressed harder, 'Tell me you love me.'

'I-I-I-love you ...'

Tears didn't cease after he let her fall, humiliated, degraded, unable to breathe. Samantha drew her knees to her chest, wrapping her arms around them. She tried to stop her tears.

She whispered, 'Sing a Rainbow' to herself. She prayed for help, desperate for warmth, wipe all of him away. She felt him hurting her, killing her.

Sam saw his silhouette, felt the wind on her neck, whispering.

'Samantha ...'

Rebecca Dale (14)
Coundon Court School & Community College

Daydream

(Inspired by 'Alice in Wonderland' by Lewis Carroll)

Jonathon was growing bored with sitting down in front of the teacher and pretending to listen; once or twice he had peered out of the window to see what was there, but all he could see was pavement, grey boring pavement. *And what is the point of a view,* thought Jonathon, *without trees or bushes?*

So he was thinking in his own mind (as well as he could, for the hot stuffy room made him feel very uncomfortable and quite drowsy), whether the pleasure of drawing a caricature of his teacher would be worth the trouble of leaning forward and finding a pencil, when suddenly a pink frog with white feet ran through the centre of the classroom. There was nothing so very remarkable in that; nor did Jonathon think it so very much out of the way to see the frog wearing a pair of silver gloves. (When he thought about it later, he realised it should have occurred to him to wonder about this, but at the time it seemed quite natural.) But when the frog actually spoke, 'I'm late, I'm late!' looked around and then hurried on, Jonathon started to his feet, for never before had it crossed his mind that a frog should speak or even wear hand garments and, burning with curiosity, he ran through the room after it, and fortunately was just in time to see it hop down into a small lake that was near the school.

Samantha Phillips (14)
Coundon Court School & Community College

Death Of Scorpious Grumbledee

(In the style of Adam Roberts)

The morning sun shone onto the mud-stamped patio scattered with birds cooling off the night-cold tiles. Around the corner gallivanted the bad omen of the neighbourhood, one that was said to resemble those seen in horror films, Master Grumbledee; he stormed into the garden in a raging fit grasping his soulmate, the only thing that mattered to him, Teddy. He ran in a hesitating motion up to the patio, he drew back his hammer-like foot, protected by the most ghastly-sized boots to ever have been seen and walloped the poor bird. It soared over the ivy-twined fence littered with nails and barbed wire; already gashed and letting out cries, it landed on a rusty fork left after a drunken party he had ruined the previous night.

The bird let out a cry of distress as heard from a cat being de-fleaed and Master Grumbledee was content. He slumped back into the shabby lump of wood he called a house, his hair fluttering back in the wind against his bulging veiny head, his long, yet to be cleaned, army-like jacket stretching down to his ankles. As he entered back through the door he could just hear the bird let out one final cry; he slouched on the sofa with a smirk on his face and so did his teddy …

Daniel Jelley (14)
Coundon Court School & Community College

The Cursed Kingdom

In the middle of the desert a great castle was built that was over 1,000 feet high. A great king lived there named Hortonne, King Hortonne. He had a son named Larrotte, who became stronger after his father died.

Larrotte became King of Kendle, a kingdom on the island of Kolloway. He ruled for three years until, Saroseth, one of Hell's demons, returned after 5,000 years.

King Larrotte and his army battled it out, good versus evil. Larrotte became a hero. They had a feast that night to celebrate King Larrotte's victory.

A year passed and Saroseth had returned, but this time, bigger, meaner and stronger. Also, with the feared and dreaded Triossadonne. Triossadonne was a mean and creepy little creature who killed people in their sleep and attacked, killed and ate people during the day.

The people of Kendle were terrified and ran out of the kingdom and were left to fight the goblins of Saroseth's castle.

King Lorrotte defeated the evil Saroseth and brutally killed Saroseth's trusty and loyal partner after a long and hard struggle. Larrotte was finally killed by a goblin, and left the kingdom with just a whisper of his words.

As for the goblins they were condemned to Hell by Larrotte's god, Fhoneous Lomattes.

Melody Hall (14)
Coundon Court School & Community College

Chloe's Inheritance

Chloe Mannings was a very unfortunate child. She inherited vast jealousy from her father and deep love from her mother.

This sweet young girl couldn't take it that her mother was deeply in love with her father and grew jealous because she believed that all the love in the world should go to her.

When Chloe met Shaun it was love at first sight. Unfortunately, he was engaged to a beautiful woman called Miya. Chloe tried to win over Shaun but he wouldn't have it. It was then Chloe realised that the only way to gain Shaun's love was to kill Miya.

One dark, gloomy night, Chloe was out on the loose, with a vengeance to kill. She opened the wooden door to the homely cottage and crept upstairs. Entering the enchanted bedroom, she watched the beautiful couple sleeping in harmony. She staggered towards Miya and gently raised her hand, sweetly let go and the knife stabbed her in the heart. Then Chloe fled to the door, blew Shaun a kiss and left.

Shaun awoke to face the most horrendous scene. His dear fiancée, Miya, was dead. He wept for days, he couldn't accept that the love of his life, the one he cherished the most, was dead.

Chloe approached Shaun a week later, but all she could say was, 'Oh well, you'll get over it! Now you can marry me!' with a huge grin on her face. From that moment on, he knew Chloe was the killer and vowed never to talk to her again.

The curse of Chloe's inheritance had blocked her path to love - forever.

Georgina Holt (13)
Coundon Court School & Community College

A Day In The Life Of A Cardboard Box

I was once a tall tree, standing proudly surveying the land that was my own, my roots spread for miles.

Suddenly I felt a sharp pain go down my trunk, then I realised I was going to be no more! I plummeted to the ground taking out other trees, I screamed, *'Timber!'*

Soon after, I woke, with a strong breeze rustling my leaves. I struggled to open my eyes to find that I had been crammed into the back of a truck with my siblings. I felt my sap oozing out of my trunk like blood from a slit artery.

Before I could say my prayers I was sliced and diced into a cardboard box. They sent me to a Samsung factory where I was labelled and they stored a 46-inch plasma TV in me. Soon after I was carted off in a lorry and distributed to Comet.

Here I stay waiting to be bought, dreaming of my glorious and tragic past.

Steven James Du'Mont (14)
Coundon Court School & Community College

Myths And Legends - The Tragedy of Troy

The city of Troy amazed the ancient world. The citizens of Troy were encased in the city surrounded by very high walls. This made the city of Troy impenetrable from the outside, but once inside, the city would be very vulnerable.

Troy was once the ally of Greece for many years but when the princes of Troy, Paris and Hector, came to Sparta to visit the king of Greece, Paris fell in love with Helen, the wife of the king. Helen also fell in love with Paris. They ran away together to Troy.

When the king realised that Helen had run away, he called together the armies of Greece and they sailed towards Troy.

When the battle began there were heroes on both sides. On the side of the Greeks, there was Achilles. Achilles was a demi-god; he was the son of Zeus and Athena. He was made stronger by being dipped in a magical river. This made him invincible but the only point that wasn't touched by the water was his heel. This was where his mother had been holding him.

On the side of the people of Troy was Hector. Hector was fearless. He wore hardly any armour.

After fighting for seven years, the Greeks left all of a sudden. When a Trojan patrol found that all the Greeks had left but one, they celebrated. The Greeks said that if they took their horse into their city they would win the war. Believing this, the Trojans were fooled. The horse was filled with the strongest Greek fighters, including Achilles. In the dark of night, they came out of the horse and killed every citizen of Troy.

Liam Doyle (14)
Coundon Court School & Community College

The Fire At Number 31

The flames licked at the unprotected faces of the scared children. The fire danced over the room like a raging bull trying to shake off his rider. The heat absorbed the energy from the small children's bodies. Smoke filled the lungs of the kids pulling them into a deep sleep.

The sirens roared as the great red beast charged towards the towering flames raging over the small house. The fire engine flew past the cars that were dwarfed by it. As the beast turned the corner to confront the fire, the motley crew realised the sheer intensity of the blaze.

The men unpacked the long hose which seemed to slither from the belly of the engine like a great white tail. A plump, short officer grappled with the hose and with the help of a tall, skinny man, they started the water. Like the ultimate battle, the water struggled against the fire. The blaze seemed to be winning until more great red beasts rounded the corner. The tall flames were now being out-powered by the new snake army.

A group of officers charged the door like a human battering ram. The door cracked from the strain of the ram. The men then split up to find out whether anyone was still in the building. Soon the children were found in a small room where some flames still danced and black smoke choked the air. Unconscious, the kids did not protest to their rescue. The officers took the children out of the house into the cool street where they were rushed away. Smoke drifted from the battlefield and the red beasts roared away in triumph.

Oliver Holmes (14)
Coundon Court School & Community College

One Night In The Blitz

One dark, stormy night during the Second World War, my family and I had just settled in bed when we heard the groaning of air raid warning sirens. I was the first one up, so it was my job to run round the house waking the rest of the family.

We were running down the stairs when we felt this humungous shudder that rocked our house. I could hear people's anguished cries and screams from the streets. We tore to the back door and saw that next door a bomb had just landed. The shockwave shattered our windows, breaking anything glass and making the crockery fly.

After we had recovered from the blast, we had to make a run for the bunker that Dad had made in the back garden before he went to fight in the war. The run for the bunker was strange; it was no more than 20 yards from the house, but when we were running towards it, it seemed to be getting further and further away. It was like we were running in slow motion. Finally, reaching the bunker, we only had one bed between four people.

Three or four hours passed before we could be confident we had survived another night of constant bombing. As we emerged from our bunker we could see flattened rubble of houses everywhere and hear the fire engines' sirens all around the city.

Matthew Greenbank (14)
Coundon Court School & Community College

The Iss

Stinger the wasp zoomed into the ISS HQ early in the morning. He had had an early morning call from his boss that needed responding to urgently.

He flew through the hole in the top of the roof of HQ that was built for wasps. He landed down into a large lobby full of chairs and desks but no one was filling them.

He crawled along the lobby to find the briefing room.

'Take your seat, Stinger, immediately,' Brutal Beetle barked at Stinger, who was never taken aback by this greeting. 'OK, listen up. At about 6am this morning we had a call from Buzzy Bee. He threatened that unless we release his brother, Stripy Bee, then he will let out deadly insects from the jungle that will end the world of insects as we know it!'

Without further ado, the wasp zoomed out through the hatch in the roof. He flew off to hive number five where they knew the insects were being held.

Stinger had an idea. He would sting a person who would come running after him straight into the hive. It was risky but the hive had to be destroyed.

He zoomed across to the man and stung him on his hand. The man chased after him. He flew right next to the tree from which the hive hung. The man ran into it and knocked it to the ground, treading on it as he left.

The ISS had got rid of the threat!

Alex Jones (14)
Coundon Court School & Community College

Mr Hackney

When the doorbell rings at 9am sharp on a *Saturday,* it is never good news. But when Benedict Hackney knocks on your door, you don't ignore it!

I opened my eyes, and for a few seconds stared up at my poster collection of Ferraris and Lotus! I'd always dreamed of driving one, but never had the chance to go to a motor show or display. Then the doorbell rang for the *third* time.

I slumped out of bed and sneaked past my brother's room and went to answer the door. He must have thought I was slow as he persisted in pressing the bell, almost trying to flatten the battery.

'Joseph!' cried Mr Hackney. 'This is the third time in the last month you have hurt my plants with your football,' he complained.

'You keep count?' I questioned.

'That's beside the point, sort it, right now!' he ordered. As usual he was assuming the higher authority, though he looked the exact opposite.

As opposed to yesterday, Mr Hackney was wearing his home-made woolly jumper that never fits, and normally ends up in the charity bag at the end of the month and, to make it worse, he was wearing grey pinstripe trousers, that were very old and spotted with compost, which, compared to his crocodile skin shoes, looked half decent.

Jason Rogers (14)
Coundon Court School & Community College

Stupid Cupid!

Whoosh! Loveitt's wings dazzled as she charmed Cupid with her swift flying; he chased her like a dog chases its tail, never losing track of his heart's desire.

It was love at first … flight.

As Cupid got nearer Loveitt, he left a trail of hearts behind him, each popping like a bubble and making a beating noise. Loveitt realised he was chasing her and hid in one of the beautiful white fluffy clouds. As he got close to the cloud, she jumped from behind it and placed a big kiss on his cheek! Stars floated above his head and his eyes glowed … they were in love!

Most of the time when Cupid was with Loveitt his arrows were off target making people fall in love with the most bizarre things; *a man and a dog?* Cupid questioned himself; he went on, *a woman and a lamp post?* He was most confused, he thought it was just him being love-stricken … but what he didn't know was very important.

What Cupid didn't know was that Loveitt wanted to be bad and do as the Devil said. As time went by Cupid confronted Loveitt about his problem.

'Yes, I am the reason why your arrows are off target!'

Cupid was heartbroken, not because she had betrayed him but because she shot him through the heart with an arrow of hatred, instead of being warm and loving. Cupid turned cold and nasty; eventually he died, along with his cold, evil but once loving heart.

Chanelle Collier (14)
Coundon Court School & Community College

World War II: The Time Of My Life

Dear Diary,

Oooooooooooo! Oooooooooo!

The siren screams over the city. My mother is yelling at me, her high-pitched voice screeching, 'Planes, get to the shelter, *now!*' Her voice echoes through our small terraced house. Grabbing the tiny amount of bread I have, I run out of the house and down to the shelter.

The blitz:

I hate the Germans, their planes and bombs crowding the sky like a lion searching for anything to harm.

The shelter is damp and dreary but it is the only thing to protect me. The noise is keeping me awake, echoing in my head; my mum is trying to calm us down but her attempts are failing.

Suddenly I hear a gigantic bang! I scream, shaking with total fear; a little tear trickles down my face like a raindrop finding the earth. I think it isn't going to stop until the morning; the explosions are getting nearer and nearer; then it goes quiet. Totally silent, except our breath. We think it is over but as we walk into the garden we notice a mass of ruins where our house once was. It isn't over, I know there is more waiting to happen ...

Zoe Cluff (14)
Coundon Court School & Community College

Short Stories And Fiction

There was a shriek from outside. Mr Jones ran to the front path; a bloody body lay motionless. There was a hole through his head. Mr Jones, a highly successful businessman, peered around the hedges. A car was speeding away. Mr Jones rushed back into his home and dialled the emergency services, 'Police, thank you. I'm ringing to report a murder.'

OK, Sir, where are you? And I need to take your name.'

'Mr Jones, 789 Manhill Way.'

'We will be with you shortly.'

Slamming the phone down, he ran back out to the lifeless body. He cautiously bent down to check for a pulse. There wasn't one, though; it was certain - he was dead!

Sirens were approaching. Mr Jones was saturated with the corpse's blood. Pulling up, the police said, 'Mr Jones?' He nodded. 'I would like to take you down to the station for questioning.' They got into the car and drove off; he was escorted into a small room in the station where the interview was taken and recorded.

'Do you swear to tell the whole truth and nothing but the truth?'

Mr Jones stood in the dock in the courtroom; he nodded his head and began answering the questions he was asked. He was on trial for murder. Mr Jones pleaded his innocence. Sufficient evidence was found that went against him.

After hours of the jury debating the fate of Mr Jones, they came to a conclusion … 'Mr Daniel Jones, we find you guilty of murder!' exclaimed the judge …

Devastated, he was escorted out, head bowed.

Samantha Purcell (14)
Coundon Court School & Community College

Casino In Money Trouble

Yesterday in a press release, John Stoudamire, Manager of the Coventry Royale Casino, stated, 'Due to gamblers who we believe have been cheating, the amount of money left in the vault is simply not enough to run the casino'. This means that the money in the vault has depleted. He went on to say that unless the casino started to recover its losses, it would have to close down because it wouldn't be able to pay the staff wages.

The reason behind this prompt closing of the casino is due to gamblers winning so much money there isn't enough to sustain the casino. It is believed that the gamblers have been cheating at roulette by using laser beams to measure the degrading orbit of the ball so that they can always win.

There are six gamblers involved in the fraud. The first of the gamblers who has been named, is Andrew Devenport, who has been previously convicted of cheating at gambling; the second is John Stokes, who has been Andrews' accomplice in his crimes. Paul Siddal was guarding their car in the car park and looking after the money. Andrea Obremski was in the car calculating where the ball would land. This was her first criminal act. James Redd and Michael Boykins helped to co-ordinate the fraud at a different table to Andrew and John Stokes.

It is believed the gamblers won over ten million pounds, although this has not been confirmed.

Timothy Devenport (13)
Coundon Court School & Community College

Myths And Legends

In a faraway place there was a mysterious monster. The monster's features were not known but it was known to exist and wander barren wastelands.

One person, nicknamed Cloud - by those who knew him for having a clouded memory - swore to destroy it after the monster was reported to have destroyed his hometown and family. Cloud had blond hair and unusually bright green eyes with a minor scar across his cheek. He wore a blood-red cape, parts of it scruffy or ripped apart. He wore a metal shoulder guard and a red scarf covered the bottom half of his face. Cloud had a sword which had been his father's which had a gaping hole near the hilt, making it look as unique as Cloud did. As Cloud grabbed his equipment, he picked up his sword and felt this was the day ... !

As he entered the wastelands, he witnessed the monster attacking an innocent person. As Cloud darted to the location, the monster started to flee as the victim slumped over, dead. When Cloud caught up with the monster, it turned out not to be a monster but a person with long grey hair and a black cloak. The murderer raised his sword and swung at Cloud who was so shocked that a person could do such things that he was struck at the bulk of his armour, sending him reeling backwards. Cloud sprang to his feet then ran towards the black cloak and calmly slashed with his sword, sending him off balance so that Cloud could land the lethal final blow to the neck.

Cloud was now satisfied and returned to his hometown in triumph, his legendary status assured.

Russell Hopkins (14)
Coundon Court School & Community College

A Day In The Life Of Mrs Powell

(My year head)

It was a normal Monday morning. I was woken up by my alarm clock screaming down my ear. I went into the bathroom, still half asleep, to look in the mirror but strangely I couldn't see any reflection. I ran into my room which had been completely transformed!

Suddenly, I knew what had happened, I had turned into my year head!

All of a sudden I came up with a great idea. I ran to the wardrobe, shoved any clothes on and went on a hunt for the car keys. I jumped into the car and headed for school. When I arrived at the school gates, it was very strange as all the teachers behaved differently towards 'me' compared to how they did towards the pupils.

The first bell went; I made my way to my office, where there was a long queue of pupils waiting for me. I dealt with the queue and by the time I had finished, it was time for the first lesson of the day. My first class: Year 11. It was very weird teaching people I knew.

By lunch I had got the hang of things. The day flew by. Before I knew it, I was back at my transformed home. Naturally, I fell into a deep sleep marking work.

The next morning I woke up in my own room and was relieved to find everything back to normal. It had been an interesting experience - but not one I would want to repeat.

Kelly O' Connor (13)
Coundon Court School & Community College

Assassin

Moonlight bathed the canals. Wind whistled down the water, weaving in and out of the city streets. Barges floated silently, rocked gently by the breeze. This was Venice, the city of mystery.

Through the city streets crept the silhouette of a man. Slowly the figure advanced on a tall stone building, gliding across the water separating one house from the next. Stealthily the shadow scaled the building, fluidly moving from stone to stone.

Standing on this roof, this silhouette could have easily been overlooked. The figure simply disappeared into the darkening blue of the night sky. Only the moonlight revealed its shape, bathing it in a dull white light. The clouds rolled across the sky, and then he was gone.

Now, gazing down at the square below, he was in control. Perched on the building he waited, like an owl hunting for prey. The night was silent; the figure was prepared for the hunt to begin. Suddenly a noise broke the eerie silence. It was the *rasp, rasp, rasp* of shoes against cold stone. The hunt had begun.

Into the square walked a tall, dark-haired man. This was a very important person; dressed in a long black leather coat covering him from his neck to the bottom of his trousers, wearing dark brown leather shoes and holding a matching briefcase. This was the prey.

The silhouette stirred on the rooftop, readying himself for the kill. The end was near . . . the end was now!

Matthew McFeely (14)
Coundon Court School & Community College

Prey

The dark passage posed many threats, the looming derelict buildings, the blinking lights and dancing shadows. Every window, every door, framed horrible images etched into the darkness. Every crunch of gravel, every whistle of wind, echoed in the mind.

A dark figure, a slithering silhouette, which made the air itself shiver, stalking, the shadow crept along the alley. But then the dirty hand of the figure reached out, groped in the darkness for its prey, though every time it came near, its victim would sense it, the unnerving presence, and turn; the muscular limb would retract swiftly into blackened cover. Prey, it all came down to prey, so it had always been, hunter hunted its prey. But the world was changing. Prey had become braver, up for the fight.

So hunter would hunt, but prey, prey would return the favour. Hands would grope in the shadows, but hands would also reach into jacket pockets, clench around cold steel.

Steps would continue and be retraced in the dark. Hearing would become sharper, shadows would be noticed, hearts would skip beats, as prey realised it was being hunted.

But who was to say who is hunter and who is prey? Does the hunter follow and the prey hold all the cards? No, for there is no prey, only those willing to be hunted.

As hunter turned and withdrew a hidden hand, hunter turned to flee. The bullet hit him as he ran, his body arced and his pulse stopped, he lay still. The prey!

Adam Whittingham (14)
Coundon Court School & Community College

The Dreadful Day!

Today, the ultimate day I have been dreading. The idea of what will proceed eats at me from the inside. An artful call from my mother causes my heart to sink. This unfortunate event will transform my life completely.

Hunched within my coat, cold and damp already (probably from the anguish rather than actual rain), I retreat inside myself to help pass the time. I know this 'treatment' is needed, but why does it have to be so life altering? It's also so dark outside ...

'Must I go?' I insist quickly.

'I have taken the time out to take you so yes, you will go!' my mum replied with such conviction that I was momentarily dumbfounded - *how rude,* I thought! But surely this ordeal must be for the best, mustn't it?

We emerge finally in front of the building. I can see the placard now, although not clearly enough to make out the words. But I already know what it reads ... I proceed after my mother on this cold winter's evening, the shadows lengthening as twilight slowly descends.

The air cools as I continue on.

I enter the small door, which seems to loom over me, but I must carry on - I must.

I sit huddled, fidgeting from irritation ... time passes without my realising. 'Katie Dadic.' My stomach lurches, I stumble unwilling towards that white door; how much I want my mum now ...

'Finished, all done.'

I hate these silly things; metal shards grappling at my gums. So this is what a blasted brace is like!

Katie Dadic (14)
Coundon Court School & Community College

The End

The cobbled street was deadly silent, the sky pitch-black, as if the world were being smothered by a dark blanket of impending doom. The night was so cold that it painfully seeped into a person's bones. Not that a soul could be seen on the deserted landscape - apart from one regretful man.

He tensely walked down the road. His eyes flickered nervously from looming, dilapidated and menacing buildings to sinisterly claw-like trees. He attempted not to make a sound. Not even a sharp intake of breath. He couldn't attract what was lurking - waiting to rip him apart. One noise: his life was lost.

He walked quietly, trying desperately not to be caught up in what was to come. He'd left too late. Why had he been so stupid? He'd known what was out there …

Footsteps. Echoing footsteps. Getting closer, Breaking the unnatural silence.

The footsteps quickened. Coming for him. This was the end!

Losing control, he burst into a panic-stricken run, not caring if he made noise. He had to get away, had to outrun it. Had to outrun death itself.

He raced down the street, heart pounding and about to explode. What if it caught him?

He ran on. After an eternity of feet desperately pounding the ground, he reached his door. He quickly slipped inside - deeply sighing in relief - but something wasn't right!

It was watching him intently, a maniacal smile plastered on its mutilated 'face'.

Now it *really* was the end!

Stacey Dodd (14)
Coundon Court School & Community College

Hell Sell

Darkness or light? There can only be one winner! But the new guy is still undecided.

Within my mind no one is normal. They all have dark secrets never to be told, unforgiven lies, hidden deep down inside. Broken hearts never to be mended again and nowadays nothing ever changes for good but always for bad.

Walking down the street I see the evil within, unable to prevent what's yet to come! My people try to stop the war from coming but we all know that's going to be a big challenge.

They've made me the chosen one. Sending me to the Underworld to conclude this battle between Heaven and Hell. This constant rivalry of the good and bad, the angels and the devils.

I believe I can go to the darkness and defeat this war.

Not knowing entering the world below could be so lethal and cruel and I'm now trapped here, in Hell sell! Within my four walls dreading never returning, to civilisation again.

All I can do now is sit by and let the battle commence.

Abbie Fellowes (14)
Coundon Court School & Community College

A Day In The Life Of A Baby's Birth

I've been stuck in here for ages now. When are they going to let me out, I want to see my mum and my dad and meet them.

How do I get out of here? I know I will tickle my mum until she sneezes me out; oh wait, I'm in her womb, I have no way of tickling her nose.

Hey! what's that rope, it looks all slimy and wet, where does it go? Let's see, around, up, down, *ohh!* around my leg, up, down, closer, closer *argh!* It's on me, it's stuck to me, get it off! Get it off!

Oh no, what's that, it's so bright, there's a hand, no it's got me, get off me you weird monkey hand, what are you doing?

Oh no! Oh no! Oh no!

I'm out, where am I? It's so bright and clean. Who's that? What's that on your hands? What are you going to do with that shiny metal bit?

Ha! Ha! Ohh! That's cold! Ha! Ha!

Wait, where's it gone, my slimy, shiny rope has gone, I'm free!

So then where are my parents? Oh my! That can't be my mum, that isn't my dad, they're all big and wet, Mum is all hot and sweaty, Dad is on the floor. What's going on? This can't be right, I must be still inside.

Who are you? What's that you are holding? No! No! *Noo!* Just please leave me alone, all I want is to sleep and rest.

Chris Marchenko (14)
Coundon Court School & Community College

A Day In The Life Of A Spud

Like all spuds the first part of our life is birth. We come up from under the ground. After a few weeks we then start to grow bigger, stronger and soon enough we start to attend spud school. Unlike humans we only attend one school, but we don't do maths, English and science, we do about how we can put more of a taste into ourselves. So when the time comes to be eaten the people doing the eating will enjoy us more.

Then once we have learnt the trade of a spud, the pickup truck comes and your teacher says, 'Good luck.' Then we are transported to the highlight of a spud's life and that is the *'supermarket'*. Once we are in there's no going back. You can meet new spud mates and some you can become good mates with. You get put into a box where humans come and pick you out and then they put you in a bag and then into a trolley. Then when you get to the human's house you have a look around then you are put into a saucepan where you are cooked and eaten and if the humans say, 'Oh this spud tastes nice,' you come back as a spud but if they say you are not nice then you come back as one of them.

Danny Jones (14)
Coundon Court School & Community College

Zu

As Zu awoke he stretched his scaly arms, flexed his powerful claws and began to sharpen them on a nearby rock. When they sliced through the rock he decided they were probably sharp enough and so went about unfolding his great lustrous wings.

The night had not been kind to him after the good knight Sir Thomas Fredrick and his horde of not so merry monsters had hunted him.

When Zu exited the cave he found himself in a large valley covered by lush green trees, the sound of a river in the distance. But he sensed a storm cloud coming to ruin his picture in the form of a small army. Now Zu could hear the marching pace and he quickly scanned the area for a boulder to hurl at them but finding none started a long flight upwards.

Zu knew he wouldn't win this fight easily and chose to weaken the enemy by shooting fireballs at them. They were prepared. They started firing crystal arrows that stung Zu badly. He needed to retreat but an arrow had pierced his wing and it was difficult for him to fly, soon he was hit again in the wing, this time he could not keep airborne and started to fall. When he hit the ground Zu was immediately surrounded by the enemy who were attacking him, he swatted away as many as he could but was faced with wave after wave and soon he could fight no more and, in a flurry of flames, he was gone, he had been reborn as a small field mouse called John. But that's another story …

Sam Kiernan (13)
Coundon Court School & Community College

Me And Thorfax

Long ago and longer yet, a dragon was born which you wouldn't forget. His name was Thorfax, who would keep his treasure a great secret? He would leave a long winding trail of unreal gold, which would lead unfortunate wanderers into his claws. I myself was one of these unfortunate souls. He asked me my business, so I told him what I wanted. He said, if I could solve his riddle, I would be able to have some of his sacred sapphires. The riddle was something like this. *What does man love more than life, fear more than death or mortal strife? What the poor have the rich require and what contented men desire? What misers spend and spendthrifts save? And all men carry to the grave?*

It took me a while to figure it out. Then I realised one thing, the answer was *nothing*. Thorfax was amazed that I was able to solve his riddle. Thorfax kept his promise and gave me several sapphires. Since then me and Thorfax have become good friends. Every now and then I would visit old Thorfax to see how he was. He was starting to age a bit, but he was one of the strongest European dragons I have ever met. He would tell me more riddles, some of which were hard, and others which were easier. He told me of his journey around the world and how he met the three dragon kings in Japan. He recently flew away but hasn't returned since.

Kieron Furnival (14)
Coundon Court School & Community College

Stranded

In the middle of nowhere a house stood. Derelict. The doors hung off their hinges. The wind howled wildly as it whirled through the windows. Tiles had fallen from the roof and the walls were covered in a slimy residue. It didn't look natural, was someone trying to hide the house?

As I stepped closer the air got colder. Someone or something was lurking in the darkness. Bushes rustled violently as I shuffled towards the house. I stopped.

Silence.

Seconds felt like minutes. I wanted to go back but knew I was fighting a losing battle with my curiosity. Nothing could save me now. My entranced body shifted onwards. My eyes glazed over but for some reason I didn't blink. I didn't need to. Something else was leading me. I stepped over a rock, but how did I know it was there? Had I been there before? No I couldn't have, I would've remembered it, wouldn't I?

Thump!

I fell but I just got up. Not caring that my trousers were ripped or that my blood was drizzling down my leg. My eyes welled up with tears but I felt no pain. My hand grasped something cold and turned it, it was the door handle, and I was there. The old oak door opened with a creak.

Something warm touched my face.

My tears were gone but the pain was now there surging through my body. I was back, but was gone again moments after as I collapsed to the floor.

Amy Harrison (14)
Coundon Court School & Community College

Revenge

As the moon's beams gently trickled through the lightly dusted windows, the misty room was lit, to reveal a shadowed, mysterious, dark character seated in the lightly frosted armchair.

As he gradually moved to stand, his immaculate shoes fogged in the whirling dust. He paced towards the chattering window, his leather coat, trailing behind him. His skin-tight leathers made his muscular torso shimmer in the hazed moonlight.

All was quiet, silent as the dead, despite the occasional creak of the cottage's beams, breathing.

The figure clenched his side with his hand, as if he were fighting for his life, his hand jolted to grasp his pocket. As he withdrew his hand, a glinting, silver object followed. Before he had a chance to replace it, a sudden movement amongst the trees and rustling in the leaves shocked the man. He reacted instantly, diving and cowering below the revealing window.

His surroundings camouflaged him; a carpet of dust lay temporarily undisturbed. The ceiling low, as a child's den is. A grand chandelier hung beautifully as it glinted in the moonlight, despite lacking some of its most impressive crystals.

The atmosphere was chilling and tense, the man, unsure of what move to make next.

A cold shiver shot down the mysterious figure's spine, as his trembling fingers reached for his pocket, the object slipped from his grasped amongst the dead leaves and cobwebs. As he slowly, silently stretched his hand towards it, his eyes met with those of another. He froze. His chest tightened.

Becky Veasey (14)
Coundon Court School & Community College

Bounce

Hi, my name's Bounce, I am a reporter for Le Jamaica. I have become the top undercover reporter and I have had many bits of work published but this, this day was the *worst* day of my *life*! I will tell you what happened.

I was doing my investigation with some homeless people and a gang of thugs who'd been going round stealing anything they could get their hands on. I was dressing up as a homeless person and was living on the streets to make it look real.

The gang came and said there was a house to rob so we went to the house and we started to loot the house. I got a phone call from my editor saying I was fired, so I had to finish the robbery. One of the gang members called 'Racer' heard someone coming so he got his gun out and shot. It was a little girl he got her in the head, he didn't care. I ran up to him and shouted at him, 'Why did you shoot her?'

Then he mumbled, 'I don't know but I don't care.'

Then I took his gun and shot him in the foot or so I thought he then got his gun and shot me. I was lying there bleeding when the man of the house came and saw me there bleeding and he tried to help me, but it was too late for me and the little girl, I was paying for my disasters.

Steven Smyth (14)
Coundon Court School & Community College

How I Lost Everything

Now I have nothing, it's all gone. Do you want to know how? OK I'll tell you, but promise not to tell anyone. It all began when I took my kids to the amusement arcade, I think they're a great way to waste money. Everything was great until I played on some games, I found myself not wanting to stop, it's like everything, the sound, the lights and the thrill of wanting to win was making me keep going. After a few more hours I ran out of money and went home.

The next day I went to a casino and played on a few games, then some more and after that I started to bet bigger money until I ran out and was begging for more, I even asked my wife and friends. I lost everything. Whilst trying to get it all back I made the biggest mistake of my life, I bet the house, and lost. My wife and children had nowhere to live so they left me alone with no money, no house and heartbroken.

Lewis Baxter (14)
Coundon Court School & Community College

A Night In The Life Of ...

I am going out tonight. I am going down the stairs now, listening. I've been lucky. I've settled down here and everyone loves me. I am at the bottom now and I am out. The cold wind hits me like a whip and runs down my back. I don't know where I am going, I am just out. I like the night, I never used to, when I was back at that place. The nights were cold and lonely, with nothing but the breeze for company. The lightning would fly and I'd get really scared.

I am out tonight. I like sitting on the pavement, watching cars zoom past, with the moonlight shining down on me. And the stars, there's so many of them at night, like silver jewels on a black blanket. I am out tonight. I am cold and lonely. My shadow, the only thing round here as company. I want to go home.

It's raining tonight and I am inside on my bed. I share this with someone, she's my friend. Lightning runs past the sky but I am not frightened, no, in fact I am purring.

Lucy Gardner (13)
Coundon Court School & Community College

See What It's Like To Have my Life - Kevin McDonald

(An extract)

I woke up and just lay there for a while, I was lying in a doorway. Believe it or not this is my home. I'm 16 years old and living on the streets. I'm still meant to be at school but I got bullied because people said I smelt and I didn't wash. They didn't know I was living on the streets, they just thought I didn't have much money. I had to stop going to school because my mum always used to wait outside the gates for me to try and get me to come home. My family had quite a lot of money and I was very popular at school but no one seemed to like me when I started being out on the streets. I never thought anything of it. It just seemed like I wasn't living in a house, my personality didn't change!

If you're wondering why I left it was because of *Grant!* My stepdad, he has control of my mum and tried to have it of me. He would tell me what time to be in and if I was allowed to have anyone in the house or not. It wasn't even like he bought the house, my mum did and he came to live with us. Me and my mum were really close before he moved in with us. As soon as he entered our house, mum turned nasty. It made me feel really down and depressed. Sort of like she didn't want to know me.

From Kevin McDonald.

Sophie Baskerville (14)
Coundon Court School & Community College

A Day In The Life Of Jamie Leigh

Cold, damp doorways! That, believe it or not, is my home! My name is Jamie Leigh, my mates at school called me Jay. I loved going to school, it got me away from the evil cow that lives with me and my dad. Well, she did live with me before she told me to leave. I know it's stupid leaving home at 14, but I had no choice.

Every night after my dad went to bed she would come into my room and beat the living daylights out of me! She said if I didn't leave she would carry on doing it until I got ill. I tried to tell my dad but he wasn't taking any of it! So I left!

Now I'm on my own with no food and no friends. My life is ruined. I'm *so* scared, I was going to go back but I can't, not now. Anyway they wouldn't want me back!

About an hour ago this strange man came up to me and said I could go back to his place, I said no. He would only want one thing. But it would be nice to have a roof over my head and food for the night. I hope he comes back.

I've decided to go find my real mom. I've never met her but I know where she lives.

Amy Gardiner (14)
Coundon Court School & Community College

The Mother Lioness And The Kitten

It was a blazing hot day in August. A young lioness was wandering the African plains looking for prey. This was an important time in her life. She was due to have cubs, any day now. She was finding life tough enough without needing to feed cubs as well.

Later that day she had found shelter under a large tree. It was now that the cubs had decided to make an appearance. She gave birth to four cubs. She watched the sunset then licked her cubs and closed her eyes as they nudged each other to get milk.

The next day she went hunting again. The lioness was sniffing a piece of grass, which she had caught a scent from an animal. When she came across a small quivering ball of fluff. She swiped her paw at it gently. She suddenly jumped back when it made a miaowing noise. She patted it again.

It stood up. The lioness laughed at it. The kitten was bumping blindly about, falling over itself. She picked up the kitten and took it back to her own cubs. The cubs started to suckle again.

The kitten looked in the direction of the lioness.

She gently pulled the bundle of fur towards her. The kitten gave an excited miaow and began to suckle greedily.

As the kitten grew older, it began to think of the lioness as its mother. The kitten grew into a miniature lion.

Sadly the lioness died, the kitten died soon after at her graveside.

Jade Polding (13)
Coundon Court School & Community College

A Day In The Life Of A Jedi

Today I will give you a run through of my life as a Jedi. As I go to find my friend who has joined the Imperial Remnant supported by a Sith cult, the Disciples of Ragnos. Now it's time to kick into action to save him.

Last time I went to save Rosh, he betrayed me and joined the cult, luckily a blast of Sith lightning subdued him but then Taurion, the leader, collapsed the top trapping me and Kyle, my master. I lost my lightsaber, but now I've built a new one, I'm ready for him.

After fighting hordes of Imperial stormtroopers I'm nearly there. None of these officers or troopers are any match for me. Good, he should just be behind this door, 'Oh no!' Three Sith cultists jump down but my lightsaber techniques finish them quickly.

I walked through the door and there in front of me is Rosh cowering on the floor. I walk up to him, kicked him along the floor. 'You, you traitor,' I shout.

'No Jaden, help, I was wrong,' he replies.

'And why should I believe you?' I reply.

'Go on do it Jedi, he betrayed you!' someone calls out.

I look up, it was Alora, another Sith apprentice.

'Hmm, I am really angry, Rosh betrayed me, that's it, I put my saber to his chest.'

'No Jaden I was wrong!' he screams cowardly out loud.

'No you weren't wrong, you were weak.' I ignite my lightsaber …

Thomas Neal (14)
Coundon Court School & Community College

The Trojan War

The golden throne awaits the great king's return. The sharp spiked gates opened to the shabby public, who saw into the dazzling gardens with a tall kingdom fit for the world.

Chariot bells rang as a sparkling golden plated and highly decorated chariot rode through the gates.

The doors boomed open as a king, with a mission to see his wife, walked through the door. First he went to the bedroom, then to the kitchen, but his wife couldn't be seen.

Eventually the butler caught a glimpse of the king and told him that he hadn't seen the queen for a while. While a gasping, guilty voice cried, 'She has been taken away.'

The king's heart sank into a pool of blood asking, 'Who has taken her?' There was no reply. He angrily shouted, *'Who has taken her?'*

The voice replied and the king knew everything.

The king thought long and hard about his savage actions, but couldn't get his head over the shock. He eventually came to the conclusion that drastic measures should be taken and ordered that the army should be recruited to amend this dreadful deed.

'Phone them, at once,' he ordered the servants and it was revealed that the army would set sail very shortly, in a couple of minutes was what the chief exclaimed.

The troops were packed and were ready to begin their journey of great revenge. Bags were packed waiting for the order from the chief.

Kieran Mullarkey (14)
Coundon Court School & Community College

A Day In The Life Of Cleo

It's night and it's dark, instead of going out I'm hunting. Hunting my prey. There's a bird, let's get it.

Next morning I leave it on my doorstep for my owners to see and praise me, I get treats for this you see.

My owners are really nice. The girl always plays with me and sometimes if I'm good they put the fire on.

Today is just a normal day, you may think all we do is eat, sleep and moan, but when you're out we guard your house, we eat your yummy tuna. Yum-yum.

In the mornings I get put out because they go out the house, so I go off to meet some of my mates. Today I'm meeting Ginger and Fluffy, they're really nice, we go to each other's homes. Today it's my turn, but it's raining, so we hid in one of the bushes in my garden, I catch up on all the latest gossip.

It's time for lunch. I go in through the cat flap, go and nibble on my food, when it's time for Katie to come home from school. I go and wait by the back door for her to come and let me in. I greet her with, 'Miaow.' I love my mum, dad and Katie.

At night it's cuddles all round, I love being able to sit on their laps. We cuddle up and I get the last food of the day. I have a wash and go back to sleep.

Katie McElroy (14)
Coundon Court School & Community College

The Legend Of The Headless Horseman

Old people say that there are places that men should not go, dark places where the most evil and foul things live. None worse than the headless horseman.

Born in a small town in a forest in France. A young and charming man was hired to do the most terrible things imaginable. He had now become an outlaw, someone who will kill for money. Until his death will ruin him.

During his twenties he became a hired assassin. He was sent to assassinate a town's lord, but failed miserably. Whilst fleeing the scene he bumped into two girls. He raised his hand to his lips and went, 'Sshh.'

The girls just stood there staring at him in a dumbstruck way. *Snap!* One of the girls broke a stick and screamed. Now that the guards were alerted he ran off to hide but he was spotted soon after.

He put up a good fight and thought that staying put would get him killed. He ran off again, *bang!* He got shot whilst running away. The guards brought him up to his feet and a man walked up to him and with one swipe of his axe, his head and body fell to the ground.

Phoenix will never rest until he finds the two girls and kills them both.

Owen Emerton (14)
Coundon Court School & Community College

Cobweb's Love Story

Me, marriage I thought it would never happen, especially to the most fancied fairy in Fairy World. I'm Cobweb, I'm not that good looking, I'm tall and lanky, and have scrappy wings. So why did Lightning choose me? It's not like I complement him when I'm on his arm, he's so handsome and his eyes are like two pools of melted chocolate and he has the most fantastic smile.

We met at Fairy College, I was training to be a fairy godmother, it didn't work out though. I'd just finished a long and boring lecture about only answering urgent calls, when someone stuck their foot out and tripped me up. My fists were clenched, I really did feel like I was going to hit them but then I saw it was Lightning I'm sure my heart missed two beats. That's when he asked me out, I was very shocked but of course I said yes.

We went on a series of disastrous dates, like when he went to kiss me and I burped in his face and the time when I went face first into a pile of dragon poo. Lightning stuck with me though. I was so happy when he asked me to marry him; I flew round Fairy World making a fool of myself. And he laughed.

I still get goosebumps when I think of him and I still go weak at the knees. He says he does too. We are very much in love and are going to stay together forever.

Faye Stevenson (14)
Coundon Court School & Community College

You're In Charge

'I'm just nipping out!' called Dr Agon. 'Tara, you're in charge!'

My heart sank. Let's just say, I'm not a born leader. Last time I broke an 80-year-old's antique glass eye, it took a month's wages to pay it back!

An angry voice growled from behind the door and a large, sweating man wrenched open the door, sending me flying!

'Badsufasinit?'

'What?'

The man started wheezing and sat down. I got him a glass of water but he'd fainted.

Oh well, I thought, as I sipped from the cup.

'Wake up!' I urged, him shaking him violently. I popped an aspirin in his open mouth. It didn't work, so I threw a basin of water over him and ...

As expected, he quickly recovered and broke into a silent scream. He snatched his coat up, spraying water everywhere, slamming the door behind him.

Later an old man hobbled in.

'Broken arm?' I asked cheerily.

'It's in a lot of pain,' he croaked.

I gently touched it, and to my horror it snapped off in my hands. I went white and my jaw dropped.

He grinned. 'That's better!' he chuckled. 'I never did like that plastic thing!'

'I'm back,' called a familiar voice.

I hid the arm behind my back.

'What's that?' Dr Agon enquired.

'A new vase,' I lied hastily, pushing some flowers into it and balancing it on the table.

'Good day?' he asked.

'Oh yes!' I gushed, grinning stupidly.

But never again!

Frances Lynn (13)
Coundon Court School & Community College

Is Jonny Ready To Go On Tour?

England rugby star Jonny Wilkinson has just 12 days to prove he's fit enough to represent the rugby Lions team. Wilkinson has had a number of injuries after his return from Australia with the rest of the team that won the World Cup.

The Lions team fly out to New Zealand on the 25th May. During their stay out there they will have to play some good, tough, challenging rugby. It won't be easy for them. Some big rugby names are missing from the Lions team, after announcing their retirement from international rugby.

We can't forget that the New Zealanders are at the beginning of their rugby season whereas we are at the end of a hard season. Does this mean that New Zealand are going to be red hot and ready to play good, strong, testing rugby?

Head coach Sir Clive Woodward has had a press conference, this is what he had to say, 'The managing and coaching team have left the doors open for Jonny. If he, himself, feels that he is fit enough, then he will be more than welcome to come. Only he knows how well he is feeling'.

The star himself has spoken to the press, this is what he said: 'The operation on my shoulder has gone well. So far in training it has been OK. I have also had an operation on my knee, it gave me a lot of trouble at first, but that was expected'.

Stephanie Elliott
Coundon Court School & Community College

The Legend Of Sir Seanalot

(An extract)

In the middle of the forest lay a tiny village called Smallsville. Further ahead was the mighty King Henry VI and Queen Elizabeth's castle; they lived there with their daughters, Princess Anne and Princess Isabella. Their maid was called Eowyn. The noblest knight around, Sir Seanalot, was staying in Smallsville. His long brown hair and bright brown eyes would make any woman feel weak at the knees with delight. His armour clattered together making a tune as he rode along on his noble steed.

When King Henry VI sent for Sir Seanalot, he was always brave and willing about defending his country. As they were given the queen's blessing, Princess Isabella noticed Sir Seanalot and saw love at first sight and, as they rode off, the princess gave Sir Seanalot her handkerchief and he took it with pride.

As Princess Isabella sat pondering whether or not she would ever see Sir Seanalot again, the maid, Eowyn, burst into the room, 'Excuse me, Princess, may you please bless the wounded men with your presence downstairs.'

Eowyn was very beautiful and could have been mistaken for a princess with her long blonde hair flowing softly in the breeze, while Princess Isabella's hair was tied up in a bun.

When Princess Isabella got downstairs she was amazed to see Sir Seanalot lying down panting, with blood pouring from his leg. She rushed over immediately saying, 'Take this man upstairs, I will look after him. Eowyn, come too.'

Sean Kilgallon (12)
Hagley RC High School

Sir Lancelot - Own Interpretation

(An extract)

Once in the dazzling sun, lay a group of strong and tired knights. Men and women, tall and short, princes and princesses. All five hundred of them were preparing for a treacherous battle. Duke Opsunds, the leader of half the team, was saying his last goodbye to his tall, strawberry-blonde, long-haired fiancée, Lady Amelia. In the beautiful setting of the Sahara Desert, they rode off in the direction of the sun, of which was setting. Sitting on the beautiful calm animals, princes' and princesses' plumes were flying in all directions, and beautiful hair was flowing gently in the unfortunate event of a sandstorm. The teams went their separate ways and off to battle they went.

The battle had finished as soon as it had begun. Duke Opsunds was feeling rather pleased with himself, but suddenly his companion rode up to him as fast as he could, 'Oh Sir, oh dear, dear Sir, Lady Amelia has been injured in battle, she is ill and the only thing to cure her is the rare diglight leaf found only in the most treacherous woodland! What are you going to do, Sir?'

Suddenly Duke Opsunds' gut feelings told him to go and find his beloved Amelia, after all this could be the last time he would ever see her silky hair, hear her soft caring voice. Hastily Duke Opsunds departed from the bloody scene.

Sacha Shipway (13)
Hagley RC High School

Arthurian Legend

(An extract)

Grath McFlid was a hero, well, that was his job. Technically he was a freelance soldier, but now is not the time to discuss his many and varied titles. He was happy again, he finally had a job to do. He had been hired by King Maugh of Wales. He (the king) was a McGilligan, the 'supposedly' evil clan. However what Grath had seen of him so far was not unusual evil-doer behaviour. He had united the squabbling clans of Wales and led many successful campaigns against the English and darker, more mysterious forces.

Anyway, Grath had been hired to accomplish two arduous tasks. Namely to save the king's daughter, one Fian McGilligan and to recover the statue of Arnheim, an ancient stone figure which brings unity and victory to those whom possess it. Without this mysterious item the English swine pressed over the borders. The borders are a magical boundary between England and Wales. They are swamp-like and home to many dark, nefarious creatures. There are no known towns, in fact the only building known to exist there is McGilligan Tower, ancestral home of the McGilligans. It is said a rogue McGilligan did a deal with a dark and evil sorcerer that was to make the McGilligans rulers of Wales. However, the rogue McGilligan insulted the sorcerer, as a result he cursed the McGilligans to rule over a desolate and barren land. As it was, Grath's final destination was indeed the borders, for the king's daughter and the priceless statue had both been taken to McGilligan Tower. But, the king had not been to the tower since childhood and had no idea of its location. The only person who did was the McGilligan's old housekeeper, who was fired long ago and presently, lived in a driftwood house and was called 'The Old Tramp of Carn'.

Peter Osborne (12)
Hagley RC High School

The Sapphire Knight

A bearded man clothed in a musty brown poncho floated two metres off the ground to address the board of councillors on the pure silver platform at the last minute meeting in Shlockersville. 'Another child has been wickedly snatched from the gates of our city and cast out into the Sledgar Fortress by the evil Switchblade,' announced the short man of around sixty.

The oldest and by far the wisest man dressed in a red silk robe faced the gathering crowd as he bellowed, 'Who will rise to this important occasion and end the wrath of the sadistic Switchblade?'

Before he could finish his sentence a tall man rose in a gleaming navy blue suit of armour with a battleaxe engraved on his strapping chest and pounded through the great stained oak doors. Buried underneath, and the pride and glory of the symbol of his lethal signature weapon, was a small insignificant sentence inscribed in white and almost unreadable. 'Stanley Stryktukeel' it read.

Up swung his mighty arm as he slung his axe into his black horse's holster. His horse let out no sigh of pain just flashed through the luscious fields of barley, its curved horn, the same colour as Stanley's suit of armour, tore through anything in its path.

He soon arrived at the run down, weather-beaten hut. He straddled the saddle and pounced off at the door covering at least 10ft in two dazzling strides. He lashed at the solid wood sending the door into the wall to his left, ripping it off the hinges and imbedding it in the nine inches of brick.

He stormed through the discoloured cream hallway and began packing his silver chain mail bag with simple food rations. His shiny blue boots pounded against the floor, the adrenaline was pumping, there were just a few steps between his boring life and embarking on a fantastic journey sure to bring fame and glory.

James Reid (13)
Hagley RC High School

The Beast Of Haydon

(An extract)

The rain poured down relentlessly upon the dismal grey town of Haydon, its former glory washed away many a century ago, leaving behind sadness and evil that many feared to speak of.

No one left their houses, they were trapped because of the feared one, the one mouths rarely spoke of, but of whom all had heard of, the ferocious beast, the beast of Haydon. The beast was protecting a princess. How the princess got there, they don't know. What they do know is that to be free once more the princess had to be freed and the beast slayed.

It wasn't as if no one had tried. Many a knight had travelled the many leagues to the Mountain of Doom and attempted to free the princess, but none had returned. Rumour had it in the town that a knight had taken up the challenge to slay the beast. Opinions were mixed on the matter. The elders shook their wise heads and muttered a prayer under their breath and knew his quest was nigh on impossible; many ladies wept. 'Such a waste of life,' they said. Even so, the knight was not to be deterred, so stubborn in some people's eyes, so brave in others, but all agreed that this man seemed to have fire in his eyes. Never had they seen such determination. The knight was tall with brown curly hair which flowed down his back and shining silver armour which reflected the sun. He answered to the name Sir Crespo.

Nicholas McBride (13)
Hagley RC High School

Follow Your Dream

It was two-thirty in the afternoon and the sun continued to beat down on the hard court at Delhi Leisure Centre in India. *Whack!* The ball hit the opposite wall of the court for what seemed the thousandth time to Anita. Anita Singh ranked as 32nd seed in tennis. She had been playing for the past twenty-seven years and Wimbledon for the past six, but had still not managed to win.

It was frustrating for Anita as ever since she could remember, her ambition had been to win Wimbledon and this year it was even more important, as it was her last year.

Two days later Anita was on the plane to London and though she kept saying to herself, 'I can do this,' her hand seemed not to stay still and every so often she would rub the back of her neck as though it ached but to Anita it was a sign of how worried she really was.

The next day loomed so quickly for Anita that it felt as though just a breeze of wind had brushed her face and before long she was on the court waiting for her opponent's serve.

All too quickly it was her final match and her final point. *Final point,* thought Anita and she started to pray and as if God had been listening to her, her deserving prayer was answered and she stood completely dazed as to what had happened - but one thing which she knew was that at last she had won.

Mavra Mirza (14)
Higham Lane School

A Day In The Life Of Paradise

My name is Paradise. I have everything I have ever dreamed of. I have a big house, flashy cars, designer clothes, diamonds to die for and all the money I could possibly ever want. To many people, my life is perfect - I just wish it was.

I am a film star, not just any old film star. I am the biggest and best around. My life is constantly in the limelight. Not a day goes by without my face on a front page and I feel like the brightest star in the bluest sky. Or that's what I believed anyway. So step into my world and see that Paradise isn't all as it seems …

So here I am, on my own. All alone. I can't move my hands; they seem to be tied behind me. I am in great pain. I attempt to struggle, but my attempts fail miserably. It hurts too much to even scream now. The bruises are like bullets on my skin from where I have been taken away. *Where?* I do not know.

I sit here on a hard, cold floor, my body tense with anxiety, not knowing what lies ahead. *Why am I here? What have I done? Am I really such a bad person to deserve this?*

My senses are on high alert anticipating the slightest movement; I think I hear a sound. *Footsteps?* The sound grows, I am filled with tension. My head is ready to explode. Closer. Closer. Louder. Louder. I want to run. I struggle. I can't. My feet are bound. *Is this really the end of Paradise?*

'Cut! That's a rap!'

Lucy Richards (13)
Higham Lane School

A Day In The Life Of An African Child

Hi, my name's Muandi. I'm 6 years old and live in East Africa. One day I would love to put myself in the shoes, or should I say feet, as many people do not own shoes here, of somebody who has everything they need. I'm fortunate to still be alive, as my mother and many friends have died from hunger and disease.

I live in a small slum, with mud walls and cardboard roof. I live with my father, older brother and my two younger sisters. My mother died form AIDS about a month ago, she was 27.

I'm all alone in the middle of the night. Jaya is at work. Jaya is 8 and sorts through rubbish searching for valuables. My sisters are sharing a torn rug. Kadi is 3 and Fepi is 1. Fepi is crying, she's hungry like us all. I sit and wait in anticipation to see if any food is brought home tonight, but it isn't good news. He brought back a bread roll, about the size of my head, to feed 5 of us - it has to last 2 days. Father needs most of it to keep his strength up - he is suffering from AIDS.

I don't go to school, most boys work from the age of 5 and the girls look after younger siblings.

My father doesn't have long left now, minutes, seconds. Please don't leave me Daddy. He has gone; it's up to me now in this cold, lonely world.

Katy Grace (13)
Higham Lane School

Barry Buzz's Brilliant Big Day

Mr Barry Buzz is a lovely, kind and well-natured bee. He wouldn't hurt a fly. Barry's girlfriend is called Betty. They live in a honeycomb on the outskirts of Sugarville.

One day there was a contest in Sugarville for who was the fastest bee to fly backwards. Barry was well enthusiastic for this contest and signed his name down immediately. Betty was worried, this was quite a dangerous contest to participate in. Bees are only meant to fly forwards.

The contest was only two weeks away so Barry decided to go out and practise working on his flying and building up his stamina.

One week had passed and Barry was improving rapidly. He had nearly become as good as a professional. Betty was getting more anxious as the contest was getting closer. Barry's training was becoming more intense.

On the morning of the contest Barry was up early practising his wing techniques. His little wings ached so Betty told him to rest until that afternoon.

2pm soon arrived and Barry was getting organised. He had a numbered badge on his stomach saying number 2714.

At 2.40pm his name was called. He made his way to the starting line and Grasshopper fired the starting pistol. His little wings were beating so fast that they became transparent and smoke came off them. He twisted and turned because flying backwards, Barry couldn't see the obstacles in his way. Betty was cheering loudly as Barry crossed the finishing line. She was happy he had completed the course safely and proud that he had won!

Rebecca Rose (14)
Higham Lane School

A Day In The Life Of A Pigeon

Monday

8am   Uncle Monty's staggered in drunk again, my wake-up call. But the nest looks so comfy ...

9.15 am   Woodpecker's up, better make a move. I ruffled my feathers and took a dip in a nearby puddle; luckily Uncle Monty hadn't had a bath yet so the water was clean. Yes, I know everyone thinks of all us pigeons as the stereotypical unhygienic variety, but we're not all savages you know. We make use of the natural resources we have, we care for the environment, unlike those pollution-loving humans. Oh, apart from those hippies, I have a thing for their headbands.

10am   Food time! Well technically food time is all day (it's easily accessible; the ground's littered with the peckings) but I'm quite ... big boned so I'm cutting down. Ooo, someone has left chips abandoned ... well if no one else wants them ... *chomp,* mmm ...

12pm   Man, waddling around really takes it out of you. I finished off my brunch with a broken ice cream cone and an avenue of crumbs. As I said, I'm cutting down.

1.15pm   Oh gosh! Sally's flown down right next to me. Eesh, she's with that Claire - formally known as 'the blob that ate everything'. Yes, not only is she fat, but she has a tiny whiny voice that can only be described like those little yappy dogs that go *yip, yip, yip* all the time until they pass out from lack of oxygen. Anyhow, to escape from Sally on a bad feather day I flew away, heading for home, but unfortunately I collided with a certain inanimate object ...

1am   Woke on street, banging headache, waddled rest of way home.

Beth Warin (14)
Higham Lane School

Legendary Mystery

I reached into the gaping hole. My hands skimmed over something hard and rounded that was lying on the floor. I grasped the object and brought it up into the light to examine it. It was a ball! I gasped in astonishment. The ball seemed to be made of solid gold. There were rubies encrusted into it and emeralds glistening all around. My hands trembled, as I knew the ball was worth millions.

As I studied it further I saw words inscribed on it.

'A long time ago a creature once roamed
Our country and others too.
It was goodness itself as it gave people help
When they knew not of what to do.

But the creature now sleeps within this sphere
And might wake up another year,
But only when the humans know
That fighting is not the way to go'.

I thought about what the poem meant. Thousands of years ago a legendary creature roamed the planet. The creature helped everyone and advised them what to do, but then the humans began to fight and argue. The creature must have tried to help them but they couldn't have listened so he vanished. So now the creature is waiting ... waiting for the humans to realise their mistake.

I don't understand why the humans fight and argue like this. Well I wouldn't would I? Seeing that I'm R156 - the new sense capable model. I know about the human way of life, but I don't understand why they don't change.

Deepti Patel (14)
Higham Lane School

Quoniam Vox Vocis Dico Mihi Ut - Because The Voice Tells Me To

'Leave … now!'

Gasping and covered in sweat, Garion woke up. Scrambling out of the knot of sheets he stumbled to his washbasin, splashing cold water on his face. Now shivering, he pulled on a pair of trousers and a rough shirt.

Garion contemplated himself in the mirror. He wasn't a bad-looking boy, with sandy-coloured hair a mess on his head and soft green eyes. He was toned from work on the fields and tanned from play in the orchard. His face though was still pale from his fright.

He thought as he walked to the kitchens, that nightmare had been plaguing his thoughts since he'd turned 15 a few weeks ago. Every morning he would wake up in a cold sweat with the voice telling him to leave ringing in his ears.

As soon as he entered the kitchen the sheer heat hit him like a stampeding horse. These were always the busiest rooms on Falcon's Farm, and his aunt Polly ran them with amazing skill. Spotting him lingering, she swept Garion to the side of the organised chaos. 'If you're not busy there are plenty of pots to be scrubbed in the scullery Garion.'

Garion's eyes widened. 'Uh, it's all right Aunt Pol, I've got some things to do,' he blurted out.

She raised an eyebrow and smiled, 'Off you go then.'

At a run he dodged the cooks to escape the kitchen and find refuge in the stables.

Munching thoughtfully on an apple, Garion lay back and contemplated the roof.

'Leave Garion.' Wide-eyed he sat up like a shot. This had never happened before, he was awake and the voice was there, crystal clear in his head. 'They don't want you here, it's for the best if you go.'

He found himself crying. He was convinced the voice was lying, but it just sounded so honest.

'Pack only what you need and journey at night to the nearby village of Jordan. Some Merkians will meet you. Not incredibly bright race, but trustworthy.' The voice was strangely compelling and Garion was half on his feet before he questioned it.

'But, who are you? And why should I leave?'

The presence in his mind seemed to get agitated. 'I will explain at the appropriate time. Now pack.'

Loneliness gripped his heart as he made a pack of a few belongings and waited for sunset.

Darkness. Silence. A figure slipped over the front gate. Garion turned around in a silent goodbye to the world he had spent all his life in and walked away, the moonlight reflecting on the tears pricking his eyes.

Lischana Lane (14)
Higham Lane School

Repentance

'I hate you! I really, really hate you!' Those words were the last words I ever said to my mum.

We had had an argument about my 18th birthday party. I wanted to have one like my friend's, but better. I wanted to have the best 18th birthday party in town. And, of course, she disagreed with my plans. She wanted me to have a nice quiet meal and after party with only close family and friends. The blazing row ended with me screaming, 'It's my birthday, my party, so I can do what I want,' and her storming out of the house. She got into the car and drove off. She never came back.

I was overwhelmed with sorrow. My tears came incessantly for days after. I had never felt such anguish and despair in my life. I was totally lost. Oblivious to the world around me, I remained in my home, my safety and sanctuary. I didn't do anything. I hardly ate drank, slept; nothing. I sat in her favourite chair with a distant, faraway gaze in my glassy eyes, recalling and reliving memories from the past. I blamed myself for her death. If I hadn't been so selfish, so stubborn and ungrateful, it wouldn't have happened. The guilt hung heavily in the air, always around me, weighing down on me and slowly eating away at my heart. I was inconsolable.

My boyfriend tried to help. He was always there for me, looking after me. He brought me out of my dark solitary existence, soothed my heartache and dried my weary eyes.

But it wasn't enough. He couldn't save me, no one could. My soul had already died.

Kimberley Jones (14)
Higham Lane School

My War

Bang! The ground around my feet shook as the enemy's shell exploded, about 200 yards away from me. It was morning, but I felt ready for bed. I hadn't had a wink of sleep, as the shelling was relentless.

Field Marshall Hughes had just given me my orders for the day. Scouts had reported that there had been a lot of movement behind the enemies' lines and there were strong suggestions that they were gearing up for their biggest attack yet. My instructions were to hold the line and to push them back.

Suddenly the shelling stopped. There was a strange silence - one that I had not heard for a while. We put our heads over the trenches, and then the crackling of machine guns boomed out - it had started.

Whistles and cheers rang out as the advance got underway. We were ready for them. We had trained snipers all across our ranks and I wasn't a bad shot myself.

I was fighting alongside my younger brother Brian. I could see the fear in his eyes, but don't get me wrong, I was scared too.

They were now in range of our guns. We opened up our fire.

Our shooting was paying off. The enemy looked like they had hit a brick wall and there was no way around.

Suddenly the tables turned and they broke through our defences. Most of my regiment were shot, but I escaped to fight in numerous other battles and was finally awarded the Victoria Cross for my services to England.

James Goodyear (14)
Higham Lane School

A Day In The Life Of A Mouse

I was woken up again by my owner today. He came downstairs shouting his head off at something I couldn't understand. It's always the same; I'm dreaming away about a life long supply of cheese when he comes in and ruins it all. He shoves some food in my cage and without a second glance at me, he runs out of the door. For all he cares I might as well be invisible. I hate him.

Like I said, this day was like any other, apart from one thing that was about to change my life forever.

I noticed that in his rush he'd forgotten to shut my cage properly. This was my chance to get away. After ten minutes of searching I finally managed to find an open window and climbed out of it.

I ran up the path and realised that I didn't really know where I was going. I decided to go right, after all, what could go wrong. If I'd have known then what was coming next I would have chosen left. I was walking up an alley when I spotted my worst nightmare - cats!

I tried to get away but it was too late, one of them grabbed me by the tail and was pulling me closer to my death. *This is it,* I thought, *I'm going to die.*

I didn't die though. Luckily for me, a dog came around the corner at that precise moment. The cat dropped me in fright and I ran as fast as I could until I came to a field. At last I was free!

Kerry Raynes (14)
Higham Lane School

A Day In The Life Of A Chav

I woke up feeling dazed from the night before; last night had been my last day of school. I rolled downstairs, still with a headache, to see the wiry figure of my mother.

'Kevin,' she called, 'I've made your breakfast and your clothes are over there. I've got to go get my benefit, bye.' She turned as she left the house. 'Don't twock my fags!'

I ate my chips that my mum had left and got dressed; resting my cap on the edge of my head, my sovereign and my favourite football socks. Now ready I thought, *time to head to the job centre.*

I began to fidget in the tight chair as the job centre bloke began to quiz me. 'So what type of jobs are you looking for?' he said. 'What GCSE grades did you get?'

'Well, I could spell fudge with 'em,' I said.

'I'm sorry, but we have nothing for you,' he said.

So I walked out without a job and needing money because I was desperate for a fag. I carried on down the road telling the old people what I thought of them. Then out of the corner of my eye I saw my source of money - a handbag.

I crept up behind this lady hoping that the bag would be brimming with money. In an instant I swiped the bag from her and began to run.

She yelled out, 'Stop him! He's stolen my bag!'

I turned round to look back at the lady, not noticing I was about to run into a policeman. *Thud!*

'Sonny, you're nicked!' the policeman said.

It was over and then I realised I'd wasted my whole life.

Chris Hughes (14)
Higham Lane School

A Day In The Life Of An Egyptian Princess

'Layla, Miss Layla.'

I felt a hand nudge me as I left my dream world. I opened my eyes to see my maid Kya. I smiled, 'What is it?'

'Your father wishes to speak to you.'

I rolled my eyes. My father, Pharaoh of Egypt, the most respected man in the land, and the most big-headed meany too, but I would never say that aloud. I dragged myself out of bed, got changed and went into the Throne Room. I saw my father sitting, head high, with all his pharaoh ornaments. *Great!* I thought, sarcastically. I walked into the room. He nodded his head in acknowledgement. *What a joke,* I thought. He stood up. 'Layla, I'm sure you know you're turning into a woman?' He took a sharp breath. I had an idea where this was going and I didn't like it at all. I turned away from him. He carried on. 'Do you remember my very good friend Ali?'

I looked at him, now I was scared. 'Yes Father,' I replied.

He came closer, his gaze became intimidating. 'He is my good friend and wishes me to help his son Halim, a fine educated young man, find a wife.' He smirked and raised his eyebrows.

The words hit me, I became numb. My blood turned cold. My head spun. A wall formed between me and everyone else. My precious dreams shattered like breaking mirrors.

I heard footsteps in the distance coming closer and closer - I closed my eyes.

Farhanah Mamoojee (13)
Higham Lane School

Riddle Me This

I walk every day. Every day and sometimes even nights. People usually say that I smell cheesy. I get kicked about and nobody even notices me. They make me kick a ball, ride a bike, they even make me walk through big muddy puddles. I once got thrown across a football pitch and I hit someone's big bony head.

At least I have one advantage - I have a twin brother. He makes me feel safe and he always keeps me company. My twin is left-footed and I'm right. He was much cleaner than me and he didn't get as smelly and as dirty as me.

When I was ripped and torn, my twin looked in a fairly good state. I got shoved in a horrible cupboard, but the worst thing of all was being split up from my twin.

When I eventually got let out, they slung me down and I landed in a corner by the wall, piles of other things stacked upon me. There was no chance at all of me finding my twin now. Everyone forgot about me. I felt lonelier than ever. And then … and then … I was chucked.

Answer: Shoes.

Charlotte Rogers (12)
Hodge Hill Girls' School

Stone Fairy

Once upon a time there was fairy called Clara. She had beautiful, glittery wings and lived in a faraway fairy village. Clara was only four and was a beginner, but one day she decided to have fun.

So off she went, early in the morning. She began to throw all her old fairy dust around the village. At the end of the day she began to feel tired and unwell, so she stopped for a rest. She fell asleep under a willow tree and throughout the night she slept, while all the animals came out.

Clara woke up in the morning as a fresh fairy, but she felt different. Clara had no fairy dust left. But then she decided to turn into a bad fairy and destroy the village. She threw all her bad dust around the village and it turned into stone. Clara was bored and moved to a different village, not knowing that she would turn it into stone. After that she became the 'stone fairy'.

Claire King (13)
Hodge Hill Girls' School

Friends Forever

Amy and I are best friends. We always have been. One day I thought she replaced me with someone else. That was ages ago. I'll tell you what happened.

One day, in the winter, I phoned Amy and asked her if she wanted to go out to play on our bikes in the park. She said she had other plans. I was so upset - she never said no to me or put me behind anyone else! I kept wondering what other plans she had.

The next day, I went over to her house in the morning so we could walk to school like we always do. But today she told me her next-door neighbour was walking with us. I was so upset! She must have gone to the park with her the day before! She was talking to another girl!

When we got to school, a break time, she played with her. When we had to pair up to write a 250 word story, she paired up with her! I tried splitting them up but they were stuck together like glue! I have to admit, I was jealous! I couldn't take it anymore. I went and told Amy that she wasn't paying any attention to me and was replacing me.

'No way. Her grandad died from a heart attack a week ago and it was her first day back at school, so my mum told me to look after her! You're my best friend forever!' she said.

Samiya Hussain (12)
Hodge Hill Girls' School

The Jewellery

It was raining outside so I was stuck inside. My friend Emma came over and we started playing dress-up games. Then I saw my mum's necklace, so me and my friend got it out of the box and started playing with it. When we had finished playing, I didn't realise Emma had put the necklace in my dress-up box.

A few weeks later, my mum was looking for the necklace and I started to panic because I couldn't find it. My mum thought it had been stolen so she rang the police and they came. I was getting really worried.

The man from the police started doing fingerprints on the box where the necklace was. When he'd finished he said the fingers were too small to be an adult's, so they said they would call tomorrow. When they went my mum was really frustrated and started to look everywhere. When she looked in my room, she found the necklace, shouted at me and went downstairs to have a cup of tea. In the morning she called the police to tell them she'd found it.

Faybian Taylor (12)
Hodge Hill Girls' School

DIY Disaster

I awoke to the sound of my dad banging away, using the hammer to bang off the remaining plaster I guess. I groaned - after all, it was Saturday. My eyes were half shut. The clock on the bedside table was ticking away. I pressed the light button so I could see what time it was: 7am. What would the neighbours think of us?

I was trying to go back to sleep when Dad started to use a chisel, *ding, ding, ding.* I groaned again. I put my headphones on and I could still hear the chisel, *ding, ding, ding.* That chisel was getting on my nerves - there was no use putting on my headphones.

Suddenly there was a loud bang. I quickly jumped out of my bed and put my slippers on. I opened the door and ran to the other room. Dad was on the floor in pain and agony. I called, 'Dad!' several times. 'Dad, Dad, Dad!' Dad didn't reply.

I was panic-stricken. Dad wasn't talking. I quickly went downstairs to the phone and dialled 999 and asked for an ambulance. After a few minutes the ambulance had arrived at my house. I quickly opened the door and the doctors took Dad. Dad was okay after a few days. So I guess I'll call it 'DIY Disaster'.

Atiyah Ghulam (12)
Hodge Hill Girls' School

The Accident Which Changed Everything

The church bells were ringing and everything was fine and well, apart from the fact that the bride was late. The groom stood there wondering where she was. He was thinking if she had changed her mind.

'She loves you,' said Mary, the bride's mother.

The bride ran into the church and shouted, 'Someone call an ambulance!' She was crying, all her mascara had run and her lipstick was smudged. She ran straight to her mum.

'What happened darling?'

'Dad - he, he had a c-c-car accident.'

'What! Where is he?' she shouted.

Mary started crying herself. She followed her daughter as she ran out and everyone followed. Some shocked, some terrified about what had happened.

Then everyone looked at the overturned car and the lorry that had crashed into it. Then a man called James noticed there was petrol leaking from the car. Suddenly the car blew up. Mary collapsed on the road and started to cry. The bride went over to comfort her when the ambulance and fire engine came into view.

Everyone took a step back and after a couple of minutes they went inside to recover from the shock, while the bride and Mary stayed in the exact same position. They both hoped that the bride's dad would get better and they both wished there was something they could do, but they were powerless. They watched as the fire was being put out.

Priya Minhas (12)
Hodge Hill Girls' School

The Fantastic Day

It was morning already. The sun was shining. I entered my living room, switched on the television and got the remote. I pressed the red button and suddenly … I was in a different world. It was like a dream but it was real.

I was in Albert Square with the fantastic great actors of 'EastEnders'! I was absolutely speechless - I was there in the middle of the square. Then from nowhere the director came and said to me, 'Would you like to act in an episode of EastEnders, as a family member of the Moons?'

Then without thinking I said, 'Yes!'

The director showed me around the square and I met the actors, like Alfie, Kat, Nana, Danny and Jake. They were the main people who I would be shooting my scene with. I was excited to be the lucky one to be chosen.

Then the time came to practise, I was so nervous that I nearly fainted, but with all the actors around me I couldn't waste time. I was pretty good - well, most people said that. After having lunch with the actors (which was great) it was time to go and act. I was over the moon to be on TV.

When I had finished acting, it was time for me to get autographs from all the EastEnders' actors. Once I had done that I said goodbye to my favourites. It was time for me to go home and watch EastEnders!

Henna Aliya Hussain (12)
Hodge Hill Girls' School

Thunderchild

As I got out the house I saw the Martians shooting at everything that came in their sight. Suddenly a Martian machine aimed its hand of blazing flames and was about to shoot me. Luckily there was a river close to me. I jumped in - then the deep shimmering water hit me. There was a riverweed in my eyes. I went up to shore and saw the Martians walking in the river, the water barely coming up to their knees. Could this be a dream? *No!* It couldn't be - it seems too dangerous to be a dream.

Bang! I heard the thunderchild shooting at the Martian machines. They were having a terrible battle. Then I saw my family on a steamer. Right when I saw them, I was shoved away.

Suddenly there was a loud and horrible noise, 'Ulla'. I turned around and saw the Martian machines aiming and shooting at the huge and enormous battleship. Then the thunderchild started sinking, they had burnt the thunderchild's heart out. The Earth belonged to the Martians. That was our last fighting machine. There was a loud cry of happiness from the Martians.

In the distance, I could see the boat that my family were on - it had reached safety, which was a relief. There were cylinders all over the skyline turning the sky green. I felt so lonely and desperate. The next day I woke up and saw the Martians lying dead on the floor. The human blood had killed them.

Asma Mahmood (13)
Hodge Hill Girls' School

The Cup Finals

It was Saturday morning. The alarm clock went off at 7am. I jumped out of my bed and ran down the stairs. It was such a sunny morning. Today was the cup final for the girls' football team.

I was in the Birmingham City team - I was a goalie. I was nervous and at the same time excited. The team had spent four weeks training with my coach Danny. I had to leave the house at 10am sharpish, the football match was taking place in Liverpool stadium. 10am came, me and my family got in the car and drove off. We finally got there at 11.30am.

My family wished me the best of luck, then I went in the changing rooms to meet my team. We were all looking nervous. Our coach Danny said some words and wished us the best of luck.

We all stood in front of the doors that led to the football ground. Three … two … one … the doors opened, the crowds were roaring. There were thousands of people. We were playing against Manchester girls' football team. I was confident we were going to win.

Our team had a bad start to the game; the other team had already scored one. Half-time came. The match began again. Score! We'd scored a goal! The crowd were cheering. With five minutes left, we had to score another goal … Score! We scored a goal again! Three … two … one … the game finished.

We were extremely pleased we had won the cup finals. We were champions!

Amena Iqbal (13)
Hodge Hill Girls' School

The Dream That Reveals The Decision Of Fate

The dark figure ran across the empty room and past the clock that struck midnight. You could tell it was a man from his figure. He was quiet. The Nike sign on his shoes shone as moonlight hit it. When his hand reached for the door, it revealed his silver watch and scar.

I woke up sweating, third time I'd had that same dream. The time was 12.01 past midnight. I stayed awake till 7am. I got up for work and got dressed. The badge on my shirt read: 'DI Katie Collins'.

At work the atmosphere was calm, after yesterday's successful case was solved. We had another case about a woman who mysteriously was murdered at midnight. A new person joined our team, DI Mark Cliff, new and on the case.

The dream repeated. I recognised the woman. it was the woman whose case I was solving. I had to tell someone.

My friend DI Stuart Knight was ill, so I went straight to Cliff's house. He went to answer the phone and it was then I saw the Nike trainers. I ignored them but when he came back, as he sat down, I saw the silver watch and scar. He had killed that woman. I asked him and at first he denied it, but then he told me.

'Fine, she found out that I let prisoners go in exchange for money and now you know this, I'll have to kill you too.' He spoke firmly.

Stuart Knight suddenly burst in and arrested Mark Cliff.

Good thing that I had pressed the call button on my phone. Stuart had heard Cliff. Again we had solved another case.

Sawera Bukhari (13)
Hodge Hill Girls' School

The Dangerous Dinner

Why do parents act like children? I always thought that parents were always dull, strict and boring. That was how my parents used to be. Note I put, *used!* Things started changing at dinner on Friday night.

Mum made my favourite dish, chicken tikka masala. Dad was supposed to be home by 7.00 but it was already 7.50. Mum and I were waiting in the kitchen with the dinner on the table. I looked at Mum. She was biting her nails, waiting. I was starving and the smell of the tikka masala was overwhelming. Another half an hour passed until we could hear the front door opening.

'Sorry I'm late, but I had some case notes to go over,' Dad said, as he came into the kitchen with his briefcase in one hand.

I looked at Mum. I could tell she was trying to stop herself from being angry.

'We've been waiting here for an hour!' Mum yelled, as her voice echoed across the room.

'I said sorry. Okay?'

'Sometimes 'sorry' isn't good enough,' Mum snapped.

'You mean 'sorry' isn't good enough for you,' Dad shot back and with that, he slammed the kitchen door shut.

Mum took a glance at me. 'Oh Chris, what have I done?' she cried, trying hard to stop tears rolling down her cheeks.

I knew exactly what to do - the next night, I made them dinner and gave them time to catch up with one another and solve their differences. After all, they are adults, aren't they?

Aisha Ghafoor (12)
Hodge Hill Girls' School

Magical Book

I was at the library looking for some books, when I came across a mysterious book. It didn't look like a normal book, but I was very curious to read it. I started reading. The story was unusual. Things started to get very strange.

One night, reading the book, the little boy in the story had a fight at school, he was having a terrible day. Walking home, I had a fight too! I was worried that my life was being run by the book! *It can't be read!* I thought. I ran home immediately to finish the story.

The little boy in the story got locked in his house; strangely, my house. Keys had gone! I was locked in! I panicked, shut the book and locked it away. Each night I kept receiving notes through my letter box. *Bang!* From nowhere the box banged on the floor. There was a note saying. 'You must read for this disaster to leave your life. You are the character in the story! Ha-ha!'

My parents then arrived, I told them what had happened. They told me it was a dream. Suddenly there was a loud knock. It was not a neighbour, nor a friend. Nobody was there. I looked and there was a note: 'The little boy in your story is going to be killed'. I ran upstairs fast.

The story had ended and *bang!* A gun fired through my heart! I fell on the floor. My death was a mystery to everyone!

Jessica Ahmed (12)
Hodge Hill Girls' School

Why Didn't You Tell me?

Have you every found something? Something you weren't supposed to find?

One evening Rochelle decided to camp out in the garden, and invited her best mates. They were all sitting around the 'campfire' (actually it was a pile of wood, with candles around it), eating marshmallows.

'I'm bored, let's go on an adventure,' moaned Jake.

They all set off, with their candles and torches, walking around the garden. It wasn't a garden, actually, more a small field. Off they went but after ten minutes, Stacey tripped and twisted her ankle. As true good friend, Jake and Thomas helped Stacey to walk.

For a strange reason, Stacey was puzzled at why she'd fallen over. 'Hey guys, come over here, look at this hill, has this been here forever?'

'Yeah, I've asked my parents about it, but they just change the subject.'

The digging soon began. After an hour of digging, they came to a halt. They found a small wooden box. The first thing Rochelle did was run to her parents to ask some questions.

They soon found out that inside the box there were photographs of Rochelle's sister. Apparently, Rochelle's sister died when she suffered from a hole in her heart.

Rochelle's parents explained that they didn't want to worry Rochelle, and that's why they buried the box in the garden, so it would be close to all their hearts.

Sana Jamil (12)
Hodge Hill Girls' School

The Quest - Finding Teddy!

I was sitting on the changing mat alongside Teddy, when Mommy announced that we were going into town to do some shopping. Teddy and I would play whilst Mommy was buying things.

Mommy strapped Teddy and I into the car seat and off we went to the shopping centre. When we got there Mommy held my finger and I held Teddy's hand. While Mommy tried on some shoes, Teddy and I wandered off near the toys, pillows and fluffy things. Everything there was nice and white. I felt sleepy so I closed my eyes.

When I opened my eyes, I was safely strapped in my buggy. Mommy had obviously gone and found me and Teddy, except she hadn't found Teddy. I couldn't see him anywhere. I had lost him. *Oh no!*

I had to go and find him, so when Mommy wasn't looking, I slowly jumped out of the buggy and tried to find my way back to the fluffy pillow place. I finally found the fluffy pillow place - there was no sign of Teddy, so I asked a toy soldier.

'Your teddy! I saw him over there,' the soldier pointed to the place where all the dolls were kept.

I crawled all the way and there he was looking all worried. Just as me and Teddy were about to head off back to the buggy, Mommy found us again.

Zakia Sultana (12)
Hodge Hill Girls' School

The Fantasy Dream

'A long time ago, when I was a little girl, I used to know a girl who told me her fantasy dream, which actually became true,' explained Grandma.

'A young girl in my class, called Sarah told me her fantasy dream. It all started when her father won the lottery. Her father was rich and wanted to buy some land to make a mansion. After a few months the mansion was ready. The government asked permission from Sarah's dad if they could rent half of the building to convert it into a school. The answer from Sarah's dad was, *'Fine'*. Sarah was a popular girl in the school, everyone knew her as a rich girl and had respect for her.

Sarah's house was a mansion with a lot of space. Every bedroom had an attached bathroom and something special about it. In Sarah's dream at home times she would go to the hall and buy something to eat or drink. The dinner ladies of the school were Sarah's cooks, the cleaners were Sarah's maids and a few other ladies were Sarah's servants. They all were paid a high wage.

Sarah had her own playing room, where there were lots of small balls in which she bounced. Her life was so happy in her dream, that she named her dream 'The Fantasy Dream'. After a couple of days, her dream became a reality.

Now Children, that was about a fantasy dream turning into reality,' recalled Grandma. 'Guess what? ... I was Sarah,' she told us.

Farhat Naeem (12)
Hodge Hill Girls' School

The Unwanted Killer

'Sarah!' shouted Sarah's mum violently. 'Come quickly, we're getting late.'

'Coming, Mum!' shouted Sarah.

'You'd better!' Mum yelled back. Sarah's mum was really nasty to Sarah and she always shouted at her.

Sarah quickly ran downstairs and said sorry to her mum. She was surprised to see her friend Sophie by the door with her luggage.

'Hi Sarah, surprised aren't you?'

'Yeah, I am. I never knew you were coming camping with us,' Sarah said.

'Unfortunately, she is coming,' Mum interrupted.

'Mum!' Sarah moaned.

'It's okay,' Sophie said.

Then they all set off for their journey to the forest.

When they reached there the next day, Sarah started seeing things. Seeing visions.

Two days later Sophie disappeared. Everyone looked for her, but she still wasn't found. The camping trip was meant to be fun but it was going wrong.

Someone is messing up this trip. Who can it be? thought Sarah.

Tony, Sarah's pet dog, was barking the whole day that Sophie went missing. Sarah knew that he wanted to tell her something but she just couldn't work out what the 'something' was.

The forest was a really nice place. Beyond all the trees there was a beautiful view of mountains and there was also the sea shimmering under the sun.

Mum and Sarah went to the mountainside and they went right to the edge of a cliff as well. It was then when the action began. Sarah was pushed off the cliff and into the water.

Now everything was clear, it was Sarah's mum who was the killer, who maybe killed Sophie and now her own daughter.

It was the end now. Sarah was dead.

Rukhsana Momotaj (12)
Hodge Hill Girls' School

The Jewellery Thief

I was sitting at home watching TV, when I heard a knock at the door. I got scared, so I switched off the telly and the light and I ran upstairs. Suddenly I heard a bang, then glass shattering and also the door squeaking. I was now under the bed. I heard the safe door being opened, footsteps too. I then heard the door close and a car go away. I managed to get the number of the number plate, it was 658 YOB. Then I quickly phoned the police. I then phoned Mum and she quickly drove home.

The police said there were jewellery robberies in other areas and also at different times, then they planned when the other robberies were going to take place. They then sent police officers to guard the house while they took the jewellery from the robber's house. Then they caught the robber and arrested him.

They put him in prison - but the next day they were shocked - he had escaped.

I also got a reward for being the only person to solve the case.

Harsimran Minhas (12)
Hodge Hill Girls' School

The Fox And The Stork - A Moral Story

The fox had recently moved house and was a neighbour to the stork. He invited his new neighbour, the stork, to his house for supper. The stork went to his house in the afternoon.

Knock, knock. The door was a dark green, surrounded with ivy. 'Hello Stork.'

'Afternoon Fox, come in.'

The stork went inside the house. The house had dark wooden floorboards. Pictures of foxes were on the wall. 'Nice to meet you, Fox. So you are my new neighbour.'

'Yes. Shall we have supper?'

'Okay,' replied the stork.

They both went to the dining room where the table was set out. 'Here is your water, Stork.'

'Thank you.' The stork looked down and the water was in a bowl. The stork could not have his water in a bowl, because his beak was too long to drink from it.

After a while, the stork left the fox's house and went home. 'Tomorrow, you can come to my house, Fox, for supper.'

The very next day, Fox went to Stork's house and they both sat down to have supper. The stork gave the fox some water in a very long glass and the fox could not drink out of that.

The stork knew he could not drink out of that glass, just like the fox had known that the stork could not drink out of that bowl. After a while they talked and then the fox left the stork's house.

'Goodbye,' said the fox.

The moral behind this story, is 'What goes around comes around'.

Saima Jokhia (13)
Hodge Hill Girls' School

A Sister Neglected Is A Sister Gone!

Me and my sister, Shelly, are worst enemies. She is really annoying and selfish; I just wish she wasn't born! But I was just about to eat my words when something really bad happened.

It all started when Mum bought a beautiful dress. You see, Shelly and I fit into the same size, and we both liked the dress. If Mum had bought two then there wouldn't have been a problem. We argued all lunchtime until the evening. Shelly got frustrated and ran through the front door. Mum thought that she'd just gone out for fresh air or for a walk.

It was raining heavily outside and Mum was really worried. Hours went by. We didn't have a car because when Dad left Mum, he took it with him. All sorts of bad thoughts came into my mind. I was the one that was being stubborn; after all, she is my little sister.

The next morning, the phone rang, a phone call from the hospital saying that Shelly had had an accident with a lorry. Tears were flowing down my cheeks, I just couldn't help crying. My legs were shaking like mad. I ran to tell Mum, we rushed to the bus stop and sat on the bus that took us to City Hospital.

When we got to the operating theatre, the doctors said that they had failed to save Shelly. I felt so bad and ashamed of myself for being so stubborn. A sister neglected is a sister gone.

Maryam Aziz (12)
Hodge Hill Girls' School

The Stranger

It was a dark and stormy night. Joe was on his way home from his friend's. His house was three blocks away and Joe had to walk through several dark alleys before he got home.

He was scared because he usually never went out by himself at night. Joe was more than a little jumpy. He saw a tall man who was wearing a big black coat and black glasses. Joe walked a bit faster. After a while Joe noticed that the man was following him.

Joe was terrified, he didn't know what to do. He asked himself, *shall I run or turn around and ask the man why he is following me?*

When Joe turned around, the man was gone. Joe thought to himself, *why was I worried?* So he carried on walking. But then he heard footsteps, they came nearer and nearer. He was terrified. He couldn't turn around. Joe turned into an alley. The tall figure carried on walking.

Joe sighed, *what a relief.* Every shop Joe walked past was closed except for the pub. A drunk man came out of the pub, 'Have you got any change?' said the man in a slurred voice.

Joe carried on walking, ignoring the man. It started to rain. So Joe ran a bit.

Finally, he got home. He shut the door, but on the coat hanger was the same coat the man had been wearing.

Then Joe's dad came, 'Where were you? I went looking for you but you weren't at your friend's.'

Joe realised he had been worried for nothing.

Anisa Bi (12)
Hodge Hill Girls' School

Victim Of Death

Murder On Doorstep

Tragedy begins for the Harwood family, as six year-old-child, Katie Harwood was murdered on her own doorstep.

It all began on 1st July 2005, as Katie Harwood went to play outside, just as any child would on a summer's day.

Katie had just asked her mum if she could play outside. Her mum, Louise Harwood had answered, 'Yes, but not too near the road. So as Katie went to play outside, her mum started cleaning the house. Minutes passed but Louise was too busy cleaning - she forgot about Katie.

After a while she went to look and saw Katie. As Louise went outside, she found some sort of red substance on the doorstep. Louise put her finger on it and to her great astonishment it seemed like blood. 'Katie! Katie!' called Louise. Katie was nowhere to be seen. Louise quickly phone the police, who then came and started to inspect the blood.

This is what they told her, 'We are sorry to say, that this is the blood of your daughter, Katie Harwood'.

Suddenly the phone rang . . .

'Looking for your daughter? You pay £6,000 ransom by tomorrow or else!'

'Hello! Hello!' replied Louise, but the phone was disconnected.

Louise informed the police who checked the phone number. She discovered it was her friend's phone number. We have heard no more but we will inform you as the police investigations go on.

Azadi Mir (12)
Hodge Hill Girls' School

Rapid Fire

In Brazil, in the north, is the Amazon rainforest. A smoker, Simon Harsh, was smoking near the forest. He dropped his cigarette near the tree, it caught fire and then the fire spread rapidly.

Lee Sharp, a tour guide was taking a group to explore the Amazon rainforest, when he saw the fire exploding into the sky. He contacted Katie Storm, who was in charge of the fire army. 'Katie, there has been a fire in the Amazon rainforest and it is spreading very fast and we need help!'

'Mr Sharp, bring the group to safety and we'll be there, over and out. Let's get a move on, there's a fire in the Amazon rainforest!'

Katie and her team reached the rainforest and they could see fire exploding everywhere. Smoke in the air turned the fluffy white clouds into dark madness. The plants were turning into ashes, the animals trying to get to the river as fast as they could. One of the team members had an idea to get a helicopter and throw concrete blocks with water from the sky, and some of the team could go back and locate where the fire was heading.

So Katie and a few team members hired a helicopter and the other team located the fire. It was in the north. They dropped the biggest concrete block and at the same time, splashing cold water.

The fire ended and nothing was left, but after five years everything was back to normal and everyone was happy living their lives.

Nadia Ali (13)
Hodge Hill Girls' School

The Horse Rider And Carer

It was 4 o'clock in the morning and Mrs Tucker was up and away. She was cleaning out the hens and getting the horses ready to clean out. Mr Tucker was out getting the herd in and milking the cows, but it is Mrs Tucker's job to help the horses. She spends time with the horses more than she does at home, but the horse she spends the most time with in the world is her own, called Spirit, a dark bay horse.

Mrs Tucker knows that she has a gift, being able to talk and communicate with the horses in a different way than any other horse carer she has met. She is able to understand how the horse is feeling and what it craves. Near the area she lives, she is known as 'The Horse Whisperer', and if ever a horse needs a helping hand, the people of the town would immediately phone. her.

Glenda and her husband, Richard, live in a country home in the north of Devon, called 'The Corn Mill'. They have owned a farm for twenty years and have lived in Devon for fifteen. Glenda is a wonderful wife, who is good in the kitchen and is devoted to her horses, and Richard is a wonderful husband who helps with the farm.

Every Monday, Glenda rides her horse over the hack for hours until her horse has decided it has had enough. She comes back and bakes cakes for people coming in the morning to stay at their B&B, which they love having as they can see all the different people they get along with. She sometimes even teaches people how to ride.

She and her husband love their jobs and will always keep them. They love being in company with the farm animals and the new people they meet nearly every day at 'The Corn Mill'. But as every day and night passes by, Glenda returns to what she loves and is devoted to the most. She is 'The Horse Whisperer'.

Lauren Elizabeth Daly (13)
Hodge Hill Girls' School

The Girl That The World Forgot

Maria Garcia was always in trouble at school and at home. She always ended up having an argument with her older sister because she felt left out. She hadn't had an easy start to life. Her father had left when she was barely out of her mother's stomach and her mother had turned to drugs to ease the pain.

When Maria made it into primary school, she was the brunt of everyone's jokes, she became 'Billy No Mates'.

As Maria grew older, she became paranoid about everything and because of this, she fell into a deep depression. Her mom and her sister slowly drifted away from her and she found paradise in her music.

At thirteen Maria became a stroppy teenager who barely spoke a word, until one day in her music lesson, she broke down to a song the class was singing in choir and couldn't take it, because it reminded her of her past. As the class filtered out one by one, Maria hung on, waiting till the kids left and then she finally spoke. 'Miss I wrote a few songs I thought you might want to hear. Tell me if you like them,' finished Maria, as she looked back down.

'Thank you very much, I'm sure I'll love them. See you next week same time …'

'… Same place,' laughed Maria.

The next week went in somewhat of a daze. Maria, for the first time, couldn't wait for Wednesday, the day which music was held on the third period. A note came round for Maria to see Miss Russell, the music teacher, at dinner time. As the clock struck twenty-past two, Maria shot down the stairs and into the music room where she found Miss Russell standing there with a big grin and her arms wide open.

'My dear girl, you have the gift of music and it is definitely beautiful. The feelings you have expressed are pure and from the heart and with my help the world that forgot you, will find you once again through *music!'*

Twenty years on, the girl the world forgot has finally been found again and because of all that hurt and all that pain, she has become a top singer. Every time she feels down, all she has to do is sing.

Natalie Green (13)
Hodge Hill Girls' School

Being You

Coral was sitting hunched up in the back of a limo with an ugly yellow dress on. She was going to her cousin Grace's wedding and she was the bridesmaid. Coral loved her cousin but she hated Darren (Grace's future husband). He was horrid. Coral decided to ruin the wedding.

When Coral arrived at the church, she jumped in a muddy puddle in the hope of ruining Grace's dress. Her mum ran over and shouted at her to sit down. Coral walked into the church and sat at the back of the church. After a boring service, Coral slouched off to the reception. As Coral was stuffing her face with cake, Darren came over with a big box.

'Thank you,' smiled Coral. She ripped open the box and inside was a blue shiny CD player. 'It's alright I suppose, but I would have preferred purple,' said Coral.

'It's going to be hard to get you to start treating me like family,' sighed Darren.

For the rest of the evening, Darren looked really upset. Towards the end of the reception, Coral crept over to Darren and sat down. 'Hi! Look, I'm sorry for being so mean, I'll be nicer to you okay?' asked Coral.

'Maybe I just want to know if you're going to be nice to me constantly?' questioned Darren.

'Yeah, I will. Do you forgive me?' asked Coral.

'Yes I do forgive you, thank you!' smiled Darren.

'What for?' replied.

'For being you,' grinned Darren.

Bethany Shannahan (11)
Hodge Hill Girls' School

A Day In The Life Of A Goldfish

I woke up and noticed that my living room was ten times the size of me. I couldn't more my arms and legs. That's when it hit me, I was a goldfish! I looked around, I couldn't see normally through a bowl, everything looked distorted. The sofa looked all stretched.

I looked up and saw my mum leaning over my bowl, she was speaking to my sister. I heard her say, 'Well if he's dead, I'll have to flush him down the toilet.' I started swimming round the bowl. Mum sighed a sigh of relief.

I'm glad I'm a goldfish but it does feel weird though. I can open my eyes in water, cool! My mum sprinkled in some fish food. When I'd finished, I had a nap. I woke up after a few hours because my bowl was shaking. It was Mike, the cat. His eyes were looking straight at me! He dipped his paw into the water and then, *'Noooo!'*

Rukhsar Asif
Hodge Hill Girls' School

The Undiscovered Murder

It was a Saturday night and I was getting dressed for my sister's birthday party. I took a look out of my bedroom window and it was raining. I was going to a disco to celebrate her birthday. I walked out of the house with my umbrella. It was a long walk.

It took me about 25 minutes to get there and at last I had reached the disco. I went to the girls' toilets to sort my hair out because it was in a mess, due to the rain and thunder outside. As I looked into the mirror, there was a man standing there. I screamed and jumped with fright and he just looked at me. He had a balaclava on his head and a knife in his left hand. I ran out of the girls' toilets.

I was stuck in a crowd of people dancing in the disco and everywhere I looked he was there. I could just see his eyes. They were staring at me as if he were going to kill me. I ran outside and I kept looking back. As I turned my heard round and looked ahead of me, he stabbed me in my stomach. I dropped onto the ground in pain. The last thing I remember seeing was his shadow running away from me. I was just left in pain.

Samaira Begum (13)
Hodge Hill Girls' School

The Funeral

The coffin bobbed slowly along on the shoulders of the pallbearers, rocking in the wind. The most unstable of them stumbled. He was a small and skinny fellow with an ill-fitting suit and a sort of permanent limp. He was the deceased's son and was in part, the reason for this whole tragic scene. He had a gambling problem. It was a problem that forever called to him. He could never give it up because the problem never really had a start. He had always been doing it and it was his life.

The one next to him was the nephew of the deceased. He had only recently associated with his uncle, because he was dying and the deceased was supposed to be rich. Not so, thanks to his son. He had paid off the gambling debts and when the nephew finds out, he will be somewhat vexed, as he has been rather in need of the money. He has several problems which are usually sorted by large men overflowing in their suits. He needs the money!

The leader of the pack was the man's brother, possibly the only one amongst them who actually cared about the old boy. The shock of the deceased's death hospitalised him with a heart attack. He was out within a day because he had never trusted doctors and often said so. Vehemently.

The Reverend saw them all and understood. They were not petty or small-minded. They were all in God's plan. Simple.

Matthew Urwin (15)
Plantsbrook School

Spotted

It was the day of the party and I woke up feeling cheerful except for the pain on the end of my nose. I walked into the bathroom towards the mirror and to my horror there was a *huge* spot on the end of my nose. It looked like it had its own pulse!

Action had to be taken so I ran to my parents' room and into their bathroom cabinet to look for something to get rid of this spot. When my brother Josh walked past and caught a glimpse, he fell about laughing. I had to lock the bathroom door to get away from him. What was I going to do? I searched and searched but couldn't find a thing. I went downstairs to Mum to ask her what to do. She said she had some special cream she would put on, which would get rid of it in no time. She put the cream on and told me to wait a few hours.

Later that day, I went to the mirror to find that the spot had got worse! The only thing I could do was to cover it up. So I got out all my make-up and Mum helped me.

After a few hours of work, Mum was done. I looked in the mirror and my face was bright orange. So I went to the party looking like I'd been 'tangoed', but I had a brilliant time.

Jemma Stanley (14)
Plantsbrook School

The Morning Of …

My brother woke me up this morning. Cry, cry, cry, that's all he ever does! Morning, day and night, but I wouldn't dare complain. All I have to say is one bad word about that baby and I get my head bitten off. You see he's only three months old and was born on Easter Sunday. Mum reckons he's some kind of blessed child but I can't see it myself.

Mum works at the Perogative Bar in town at night as a waitress. It's good pay but I normally get roped into babysitting. I wouldn't mind if it was just me and my brother but it's not. There's Anastasia and Megan too. Tasia is what we call her for short, she's six, nearly seven and she's got long blonde hair and green eyes. She thinks she's a dude with her ears pierced. She's the opposite to Megan. Megan's got dark hair and brown eyes. She's three and about to start school.

I tried to get the day off school by blaming my tiredness on the baby, but as per usual it didn't work. I suppose school wasn't that bad and besides it was non-uniform day. I'd been up half the night deciding what to wear. As soon as I was ready I stumbled down the stairs and fell into the kitchen. All my lunch was laid out on the counter ready for me to put it in my bag.

Samantha Johnson (14)
Plantsbrook School

Short Stories And Fiction

I was running away from the gunfire, bullets missing me by centimetres. Then I dived into the trench and headed towards the make-do kitchens. It was morning and I had decided to take a risk so that I could get the breakfast going early for the hungry soldiers. You see I didn't want the 40 soldiers in my platoon to wake up at 6 in the morning and have no fry-up. I needed to cook 45 breakfasts; 40 for the soldiers, one for me, one for the sergeant and a further three for the doctor and medics. I chopped up 250 mushrooms and put them in a large frying pan and put 100 rashers of bacon in the next and so on for the sausages, eggs and hash browns. I then put on the beans and tomatoes and was now ready to grill the toast and this is where the problems occurred.

Making toast, a simple enough task you may think but this time there were problems. The first was that I couldn't find the bread knife so I had to use my machete, with which I cut the tip of my finger off. I was still in a race against time so I had to use plasters to keep the finger attached. I then had to grill the toast but the sausages were on the grill so I heated an enormous piece of slate with a flame-thrower and grilled the toast. But before I could put the food out, the soldiers arrived. I forgot there was an attack this morning and I was late as always.

Josh Jones (14)
Plantsbrook School

The Cunning Fox

There was once a lonely fox, he was a bright cunning fox, he'd been through a lot of adventures in his life, and here is one of them …

One day the fox was strolling through his woods minding his own business. It was a bright and beautiful morning. Then all of a sudden he heard a loud *bang!* He ran back to his lair and stood silent for about eight minutes. He came out and he started to feel hungry. He went to a place where he finds his lunch and all of a sudden, barking dogs started to run after him.

He was running and running but he could feel and sense that they were gaining speed. The poor frightened fox couldn't find his lair and he started to panic. But then after about ten minutes of constant running away from these monstrous creatures, he turned around and fought back. He swung his paws around one of the dogs' face and bit anothers' neck.

The fox then saw three men on horseback with fox-skins attached to them. They were wearing smart uniforms and he knew then that the dogs belonged to them.

He had managed to get rid of two of the hounds but three remained chasing after him. Then as he dodged the trees and branches, he ran into his lair. He could still see the dogs' noses through the gap in his lair. His heart was beating and he knew what a lucky escape he'd just had.

Jacob Pardoe (14)
Plantsbrook School

A Day In The Life Of ...

It was a normal Sunday morning but I was up especially early today as I was about to go to my final rehearsal. I got up and I didn't really fancy breakfast, but I had it.

Next thing I knew, I was arriving in the car park and I walked through the school doors and went straight to the allocated dressing room. I was sitting and talking to some friends and time passed quickly.

Now I'm standing behind the curtains for the 'good morning' section and Tamsin has the biggest grin on her face. I think she is excited!

Wow, that was an experience but I must go and get ready for the finale. Next thing I know, I am getting my own clothes back on and then I am saying my goodbyes until tomorrow. Everybody needs to get a good rest for tomorrow's show.

There was silence in the car on the way home. I wonder what thoughts are going on, but today we have had a day of mixed emotions!

Anyway, I must go and get my beauty sleep as it is a big day tomorrow, so *goodnight!*

Monique Watkeys (14)
Plantsbrook School

A Day In The Life Of Little Jimmy Brown

Hello, my name is Little Jimmy Brown. I am ten years old and I live with my parents. I bet you are wondering why I am called *Little* Jimmy Brown. This is because of my height; I am 20.5cm tall. I get teased at school because of my height, I can't help it if I am small. My mum tells me not to pay any attention to them because one day I'm going to be just as big as them.

My daily routine starts at about 8 o'clock. I get up, go downstairs and eat my breakfast, then I go upstairs and do a few stretches on my stretching machine. Then off I go to get changed and out the door at dead on 9 o'clock to go to school in the car. In our car I love to look out the window and enjoy the view, but I need my booster chair or I won't be able to see.

When I get to school I am happy to be greeted by my friends, Jack, Tom, Bob and Fred. We have so much fun in the playground when we play hide-and-seek and none of them can find me.

So now you've seen a bit of the life of Little Jimmy Brown. Bye.

Emily Ward (13)
Plantsbrook School

A Day In The Life Of Britney Spears

In the morning, I wake up around 11am if I'm not doing something. I have to practise for a concert or anything like that, I normally wake up around 8am. I hate waking up early, I get so moody. When I have got out of bed and had my breakfast, I look a bit of a mess so I go upstairs, have a wash, brush my teeth and get dressed.

Today is Saturday. Normally Saturday is a really busy day, but I don't have anything to do. At about 1.45pm I have to go to the dance studios to practise my dance. My dance instructor's name is Tim. He is such a great teacher. He makes all of my dances up for me.

At around 3 o'clock I had my lunch and then got back to some more dancing. When I had finally finished my dancing, I went home. It was about 5 o'clock.

I laid on the sofa nearly falling asleep, so I got up and made myself beans on toast. I love beans on toast, with grated cheese on the top. It's the best.

When I finished my dinner, Spot came in; she's my cat. I fed her. It was about 10.30pm by the time I had finished all of this, so I went up to bed because I had an early start in the morning.

Heather O'Brien (14)
Plantsbrook School

A Day In The Life Of A Sidewinder

I was woken by a blinding light like a torch being shone into my eyes. It was the sun's ferocious blaze creeping over the desert dunes. I lay in a coil for a while, but it soon became hot, white-hot even, so I sort of hopped along the sand in a curvy sort of way and found some shade underneath a tall, prickly cactus.

I was hungry, I hadn't eaten in a month or so. I decided to find some tasty desert rats. Well OK, they're not tasty but at least they are filling. I supposed the heat of the white, hot sand would kind of fry the carcass-to-be that was my next dish. If I went anywhere near the sand's white-hot surface, bearing in mind I was in the shade, I would burn and boil. I didn't want to die, so I dug.

Weaving my way underneath the sand's surface was a lot easier than riding the dunes along the top. I dodged stones, rocks, bones and plant roots until it hit me. The smell of a big, fat, juicy rat thrilled me with excitement. I sped up the movement. The smell got stronger, harder, denser … it was right there. I surfaced to feel the wrath of the sun's heat beating down onto my arrow-shaped head. My newest meal was staring me in the face.

It was night-time and the sun's light had only just settled its rage. I suppose that today was a good day. Although some people would say you can't get to sleep on a full stomach, not me. There was a lump halfway down my body!

Thomas Surridge (14)
Plantsbrook School

A Day In My Life

It was the morning of our holiday. I hadn't actually slept that night. I had stayed up talking to my sister planning what we would do there. This is the place we have been for the last nine summers. We go to a little town off the coast of Cornwall, St Ives, about a half hour drive from Land's End.

At 6am my alarm went off and I dived out of bed and went to the bathroom. I ripped my pyjamas off with excitement and then I jumped in the shower. I finished, got dressed, cleaned my teeth and put my toothbrush and toothpaste into my bag. I checked through my stuff to see I had everything, and I did.

We had a really long journey ahead of us so we packed a bag with tea for my mom, nan and grandad. There were sandwiches, crisps, boiled sweets (for our sucking competitions!) and a lot more. My mom and sister were both up, washed and dressed, so we got all of our stuff down to the hall, ready to go. We all had a quick bite to eat and then we were on our way.

We went separately. My mom and my sister set off for the coach. At 9am my uncle, who is only a year older than me, knocked on the door. I locked up and we drove out of Boldmere Road.

We were finally there, so we pulled on our wetsuits over our bodies which were hot and sticky from travelling, and jumped in the sea!

Danielle Watkeys (14)
Plantsbrook School

A Day In The Life Of Me

When I woke up in the morning, tired as usual, I didn't know that it would be the most terrifying day of my life.

I got to school as usual with my homies, went to registration and everything was normal. It wasn't until first lesson, when I was bored stiff, that I looked out of the window and saw the birds going crazy. I didn't know what was going on, so I asked my teacher what they were doing.

'Mating season,' she said.

I didn't know what it was, but I knew that she was lying just so I would shut up.

When it was break, I looked up at the sky while eating my crisps and I dropped them. A teacher saw me do it and came over to have a go, but what I saw in the sky was much more important.

I couldn't believe what I was seeing: hundreds of spaceships coming to land on Earth. All of a sudden, something boomed out of the main spaceship. 'We come in peace,' it screeched. Everyone shouted with joy that they weren't going to kill us all, but me and my homies had seen films like this and didn't believe them. We started hurling rocks and bricks up to the spaceships.

We then realised this was a bad mistake. It started shooting lasers at us, but we kept throwing. Eventually the aliens learned their lesson and flew back to their planet.

James Willis (14)
Plantsbrook School

Fish And Chops

It was a cold winter's night and there was panic in the small town of Erdley. It was only about 6pm but it was pitch-black. There had been a killing every night for four nights. Most of the victims were young women, but the latest one was an elderly man. Most people were trying to carry on as usual, but everyone was worried about their safety, even though they didn't show it.

Madison, Alex, Tony, Channy and Jenni were going to the cinema, and the film was set to finish at about 10.30pm. They all had quite a long walk home after they went into the film and watched it. When it finished, they all set off home. The streets were quiet and a bit eerie. Alex got a lighter out of his pocket and lit a cigarette that he had been holding behind his ear. After walking for about ten minutes, they stopped at the chip shop, then they carried on walking again. They came to an alley that they had to walk down. They set off down the alley, when Jenni heard a noise. She turned around just when the axe sliced her neck. The rest tried to run off, but the masked man sliced at their legs and they all fell to the ground screaming. He then chopped all of their heads off.

Sam Robinson (14)
Plantsbrook School

The Legendary Tengu

The Tengu had the body of a bird, but the face of a human. It's nose was what made it truly remarkable. Its huge nose could cure any disease when rubbed onto the forehead of the sick. Some would class this as a miracle, but there was one problem as the once-profound healer had fled to a distant mountain. Many people tried to go and get the Tengu to return to the village, but after hundreds of years of war and famine, it had grown hostile to all those that ventured into its lair seeking relief from disease.

Once, the great Tengu fled from its domain for a group of the village's strongest warriors came into its lair in order to use the Tengu's nose with its permission or not. The Tengu fought bravely in battle, but was eventually surrounded, captured and forced to help the sick and needy. The Tengu's nose was used so much that it eventually grew weak and powerless, leaving it what the villagers called 'useless'.

The Tengu, weak and exhausted, managed to climb up the mountain back into its lair and there, under the starry, moonlit sky, the Tengu laid its head to rest and didn't get back up.

Craig Hayes (14)
Plantsbrook School

A Day In The Life Of Christian Long

(An extract)

Christian Long, what can I say? The kid is a legend. He wakes up at about 7am, has a quick little wash, eats his breakfast and brushes his legendary teeth. After he has done this, he gets changed, starting with the boxers (Calvin Klein), then he puts on his school trousers. After that he will get his Lynx deodorant; first under the armpits, then around the body. Then he puts on his shirt and tie. After this is done, he will go downstairs, pack his bag with the day's lessons and then he will gel his jet-black, silky hair. When this has been achieved, he adds a few more items, like socks, or a blazer, gets his keys and money and off he goes, no later than 8am.

On the way to school he meets his mates at Mills, the shop down the road. They are Wiltred, Shawy, Gardiner, Pat, Morgan (Cheesy) and Jamie.

They go to another shop, which is next to the Odeon. They all usually purchase drinks as well as some sweets for the journey. On the way they discuss topics such as what was on TV yesterday or what they did.

Christian Long (14)
Plantsbrook School

Shocker

Yesterday afternoon, reports on a stray dog were coming in. The dog named Bonnie, has run away from his home in Essex. He was spotted yesterday in Birmingham and has already attacked three members of the public.

One of these victims is Sarah, aged 14, who is about to tell us her story. 'I was on my own, the weather was quite wet and rainy. I was near my house and all of a sudden, this huge bulldog jumped onto my face. I screamed and attempted to run away. He held onto my leg and ripped out a huge chunk. I was in *soooo* much pain. He then bit my arm. People heard my screams and came out and helped me. As they came, the dog ran off. I was later rushed into hospital, where I had an operation to try and save my leg. This dog has left me scared to leave the house. I am now also terrified of dogs'.

There were two other people who were attacked, but preferred not to talk about it.

The dog has been described as brown with a white tail. He is very vicious. He's a bulldog and has no other colour on him. If you see this dog, phone this number: 0784 3411111, as he may attack someone again. Also, if your dog is lost and fits this description, please go to your nearest police station. We will keep you updated. Thanks.

Charlotte Nisbet (14)
Plantsbrook School

A Day In The Life Of Myself, Thomas Davis

A normal school day starts with me first getting up in the morning, preferably around 7.30am. I then head for a quick shower to wake myself up. From there, I get my school uniform on in my bedroom and then I'm off downstairs to get my breakfast. After breakfast, I go back upstairs to do my teeth and get some money for lunch from either my mom or dad. I leave the house just after 8am and it takes around ten minutes to arrive at school.

School starts promptly at 8.40am, when my year group has an assembly, or I go to my tutor group room. My tutor is Mrs Turvey. At 9am, period 1 starts. Each period is an hour long and we have two lessons before we have a break. We then have two more lessons up to lunchtime, which starts at 1.20pm. My classmates and I get food from the canteen; either a cooked meal or sandwiches. We have just under an hour to have lunch and to speak to friends in the school.

When the last lesson finishes at 3.15pm, I have the choice to either take the school bus or to walk home, which is what I do because I live so near. When I get home, I start my homework or lie on the sofa before doing any sport activities. I then usually on a school night go to bed between 10pm and 10.30pm.

That to me is a normal school day. Pretty boring at times, but not so bad that I can't cope with it!

Thomas Davis (14)
Plantsbrook School

A Day In The Life Of Me, Hannah Kavanagh

'Hannah, wake up!' This is my mum waking me up at 7am. Unfortunately she is my alarm clock since my real alarm clock got smashed on the floor during one of my sleepwalking moments. By the time I actually get out of bed, it's about 7.10am. Then I have a wash. My usual make-up chores last for approximately 10-15 minutes, but it's worth it because I look *gorgeous!* I have breakfast then finally before school, I straighten my hair.

At 7.50am, Mum drops me at Lucy's on her way to work. Lucy takes longer than me in the morning, so we end up leaving her house at about 8.05. We walk up to Emily's house and meet Rosie and Charlotte. We end up being late for school due to us five talking all the way there.

School is usually boring, but as the chatty one of the group I make everyone happy because of my 'not funny' jokes. We usually have one self-obsessed boy calling me 'Ginga', when in fact my hair is not ginger, it is more auburn, and natural, of course. Some people obviously don't know the meaning of a natural beauty!

By the end of the day, my make-up has worn off and my hair has turned kinky. I get home, watch a bit of TV and then when my dad comes home, we have tea. If it's a Monday, I'm usually at the gym; Tuesday at Judo, Wednesday working at Good Hope Hospital for my Duke of Edinburgh Award, Thursday, swimming and Friday, nothing! Saturday I dance and Sunday I horse-ride. Pretty packed week, hey!

Before bed, I put on my pyjamas, brush my hair, get my make-up off, wash and clean my teeth. Then finally, I use toner, cleanser and moisturiser. When finished, I put on my eye mask and finally fall asleep.

Next day starts the same, but the topic of conversation is different. Usually, chats consist of talking about what happened on 'Big Brother' last night.

Hannah Kavanagh (14)
Plantsbrook School

A Day In The Life Of A Pop Star

'Wake up, wake up!' my manager shouts at 5am to start another day as a pop star. I have to get changed quickly and get in my private limo to the BBC studios in London. It's a real pain because I only get about two hours of sleep a day.

It's 10am and all the crew make me wear horrible outfits that are dreadful. Then they give me stuff to say for the interview. If I say what I feel, I'd get sacked straight away.

'Here he is, it's Jamie Wood,' said the presenter.

Here's the bit when I put on a really stupid smile, then the kids ask me really stupid questions.

'What's it like being a pop star?' the kid said.

I said, 'It's fantastic, it's like a 24-hour roller-coaster ride.' I was made to say that, of course.

After the morning show, it's going into a music show promoting the new single. There is usually a big crowd around me, which makes me feel lonely, ironically. It makes me think about all my family and friends that I'm missing. Next is my hour break, where I mostly think about how miserable I am.

At the end of the day they record 'Top of the Pops'.

'Now it's Jamie Woods performing 'What I Believe In',' said the presenter.

This is when I sing yucky pop music to a really stiff audience. I don't actually sing, I have to mime because my manager says it's better. At the end of the performance, the audience is made to cheer. I wish that I could have more control over my music and image. Being a pop star is not what it's cracked up to be.

Stuart Blythe (14)
Plantsbrook School

Dream Romance

(Inspired by 'My Heart Will Go On' by Celine Dion)

'Every night in my dreams I see you, I feel you ...'

She let her body go, drifting into unconsciousness. She knew he was waiting. He was always there, in that same rose-red room - the colour of blindness. That same song echoing in the background - an unnoticed warning. With that same look in his eyes. She knew she was in love.

'Love can touch just one time and last for a lifetime ...'

She knew she should let go, leave this unforgiving stranger. But one accidental glance into his deep blue eyes, reflecting the calmness of the ocean, and she could do nothing but run into his comforting, loving, forgiving, out-stretched arms. Never looking back.

'You're here, there's nothing I fear and I know that my heart will go on ...'

They danced together, swaying in time to the music as one; never really hearing it, never listening to its message. They clung to each other, as though it would kill them to be apart, when in fact, it was killing them to be together.

'We'll stay forever this way ...'

She knew her time was short. She was constantly alert, knowing the buzzing swarm of wasps would soon tear her body away from his, at its affixed time. Knowing that when it did, she could never come back.

'You are safe in my heart ...'

The buzzing began. He started to fade away slowly, slowly, until she was standing alone. Rest in peace Rose-Ann.

'And my heart will go on and on.'

Samantha Johnson (16)
Queen Mary's High School

Floating

OK, so here it is. All I know about myself. My name is Sarah Gorge. I'm 33 standard days and I think that I'm floating. I don't know where. I don't know how. I just know that I'm floating and that it's not natural.

Maybe I should open my eyes? I think to myself. *Maybe if I can do that I won't be floating anymore.* But I don't. Well actually, it's because I can't. I don't seem to have eyes. Where are they? What has happened?

Memories. Memories keep coming to me. I can hear a voice. It doesn't seem like a nice voice. I think I should recognise it.

Pain. Pain beyond all that I have ever felt before. Where my arms and legs should be.

Feeling. It's coming back. Someone is putting a mask on me. Then a spine-tingling scream comes from somewhere. It sounds distorted. It's mine.

An amplified sound comes to the part of my brain where my ears were. It's my breathing. Although it's not mine. A machine is doing it for me. Scratching the back of my throat.

This is me. This is how I'll always be. I wish I was dead.

Georgia Palmer (13)
Rugby High School

A Day In The Life Of A Balloon

I was only small and was with many of my kind. Each day we would watch, wait, hope for someone to come and take us with them, to look after us and for us to play with their children. Most of my days were long, they dragged on and never seemed to end, but this day was the most eventful of my life.

I awoke, cramped and squashed in the small space I shared. You'd have thought I'd have given up, but I looked my best and I was chosen! A kindly woman took me home and for once, I felt alive!

I grew up and was no longer small. I had a ribbon put in my hair and I had someone to play with. All of a sudden, I was flying, up, up, up, happy and content. I became hotter and hotter until … *bang!* My dream burst and I floated down to the ground.

Now, I lie on the ground, broken and torn. I'm useless, but I'm waiting, waiting to be renewed, restored and loved.

Emily Spademan (12)
Rugby High School

The Girl

From the moment I opened my eyes I knew it. I knew that something life-changing was going to happen to me and change my life forever. I didn't know if it would be something pleasant or shocking, but I just had a feeling that today was the day. And I was right. Today was the day.

It all happened when I was walking to school just like any other day, walking to meet my friend who lived ten minutes' walking distance away from me. I saw the same things I see every day: same people, same surroundings and the same small animals. However, one thing I saw was not the same. In the distance ahead of me, I saw a girl walking along the path by herself, calling something that I couldn't quite hear.

She was a small girl of about the age of four, with blonde hair, blue eyes and wearing a pink dress. As I drew nearer, I heard her calling for someone. Calling, 'Mummy, Mummy, where are you?' With tears rolling down her cheeks, she ran into the road, and that's when I saw it. A red car came roaring round the corner. I looked at the girl and looked at the car. There wasn't much time. I ran forward, sprinting towards the girl. I leapt forwards and pushed her onto the pavement.

And here I am in hospital, both of us alive, the girl's mum constantly repeating, 'Thank you, thank you so much.'

Lucy Owen (13)
Rugby High School

A Day In The Life Of A Child In The Year 3000

Xabier is a thirteen-year-old girl living in a mansion with three robots. One robot teachers her, one cleans and cooks, then the last one looks after her and takes her to anywhere she needs to go.

Xabier wakes up between 10am and 11am. She has one lesson every day, which lasts for an hour. This could be: text messaging, emailing, shopping, and when she reaches her 14th birthday, she will have driving lessons. These will be taken in a small electric car, in which you press a button to go, then you tell it which direction you wish to go.

At 2pm, Xabier will have her lunch, which will consist of blended food. However, this will not contain any vegetables, as they no longer exist.

After lunch, Xabier's parents will come and visit her for several hours, maybe bringing her a small treat, such as a new laptop.

At 9pm, Xabier will have her dinner with the three robots. She will then watch some programmes or films in her home cinema.

Finally, she will go to bed at approximately 12pm.

Emma Stretton (13)
Rugby High School

A Day In The Life Of Geva Mentor

Up at dawn, ready and raring to go, she showers, dresses in the famous red and white England netball kit and pulls the goalkeeper bib over her head. Plenty of carbohydrates for breakfast, before she heads off for some serious training: warm-ups, practises and plenty of water.

There are people in the world who are famous for the families they were born into or for offering to take part in real-life television shows. These people have no skill, no determination, no power. Geva Mentor does. Yet eight in ten people would never have recognised her name.

Geva Mentor is a highly-skilled person and my idol. The effort and the team work that goes into defending that goal every single game that she plays, is unbelievable. The amount of effort, training, practising and pure skill that she puts into her career is totally astonishing. One day, I wish to be like her, representing my country on the England netball squad. One day. One day in the life of Geva Mentor …

Sarah Osborne (13)
Rugby High School

Left Alone

Sun poured through my window, the warm breeze ran over my face as I woke. This was not just any morning; I was going to be searching for the lost temple of Takuta. I threw the covers from me and ran to the window to smell the fresh air. I was looking over nearly the whole of the island.

Once I was dressed and breakfasted, we were off on our search. The team consisted of me, my mum, my dad and some experts. We did this often, so I was used to the whole expedition life.

I quickly found that I had chosen the wrong footwear. Flip-flops were my choice as I thought it would be an easy stroll, but boy, I was wrong! The forest floor was covered with broken twigs and any crawling insect you could think of. Within an hour we got extremely tired and my flip-flops flopped more than they flipped! We sat for a *five* minute rest. That was all I got. Five lousy minutes! I had to rest a little longer and called after my parents to say I'd catch up. I didn't think they heard me, but I had my mobile. I fell asleep.

I woke with a fright. No one knew where I was and neither did I. I was in a wooden hut and nothing surrounded me. I couldn't get up, my hands were tied. I was in for something bad and I knew it!

Megan Turner (13)
Rugby High School

A Day In The Life Of A Victorian Servant

I awoke this morning at precisely 6am and had to put my hair up in a bun as my master, Lord Gladstone, will not let me wear my hair any other way. At 6.30am, I go downstairs and put the kettle on, pull up the blinds and clean the fireplaces. I have to make the master and mistress early tea at 7am. I serve breakfast to the children: Louise, Philip, Elizabeth and Albert at 8am. At 9am, my chores really start! I have to clear the breakfast table, make the beds, clean the taps, wash the floors, clean the toilets and dust every bedroom. This has to be done in three hours, because at 12pm, I have to serve lunch. After I have cleaned up from lunch, I eat my own lunch. This is usually at 1pm.

My afternoon tasks include doing laundry, cleaning and cleaning out servants' bedrooms. These chores take me until 6pm. At 6pm, I must set the table for dinner, then at 7pm I serve dinner. I do the washing up at 8.30pm and eat my own supper at 10pm. I finally am allowed to sleep at 10.30pm.

The next day I must start all over again. I only get paid £6 a year - all of which I send home to my mother.

Rachel Webster (13)
Rugby High School

A Day In The Life Of Darcy Bussell

Sharp, I am awake at half-four, I have no choice; my training begins at 6 o'clock. My breakfast is already on the table for me, well, I wish. Really, I have to make it myself! Cereal and milk. It's the best form of energy when you have a 12-hour working day in front of you. I know it's demanding, 12 hours, but … you get used to it!

I've a leading role in an upcoming West End production. No rehearsal is ever the same. I suppose that's why I love it so much.

Down the road and round the corner, that's my journey every day to training. As soon as I walk through the door, we have a warm-up session. You can never be too careful. *Ouch!* I pulled a muscle yesterday. No time to moan though, straight to work.

The production is in 17 days! We are nowhere near ready, we need more like 117 practices. Time seems to fly by when you're having fun, that's why it seems to be on a standstill. Apart from the two breaks we have. After the rehearsals I have a training session for young dancers, then an interview.

I don't get home until 11 o'clock. More training for me it looks like! Then bed!

Toni O'Toole (12)
Rugby High School

A Day In The Life Of A Painting

I lay there pinned to the wall, watching people watching me, studying their expressions, reading their faces. *What did I look like?* A little child wandered up to me, an expression of concentration, his eyes squinted. Then an adult came and whisked him away, frowning at me. I frowned back, but I didn't change. *Was I a sad picture?*

I looked in the glass of the framed picture in front of me. I could make out a blurred green pastel in the mist of peach ... a yellow background ... but black. Someone came and stood in front of me, their eyes wide open, their mouth dropped. *What kind of picture was I?* I reached out a shaking hand. *A delicate picture, every stroke painted with detail?*

I looked around the gallery. It used to be crowded, now only the small child was left, silently sitting, staring and studying the paintings. Then ... black.

Abigail Thornton (13)
Rugby High School

A Day In The Life Of A Personal Shopper

Meet Laila. She is a personal shopper in London for the rich and famous. She has worked with the likes of J-Lo and Jennifer Aniston. But it's more demanding than you think. Read on.

The time Laila has to wake up depends on the job. Today she woke up at 9am, as she had to pop into her office. She dresses in stylish but practical clothes for her job, including flat shoes! Then she made her way to a posh café to meet her client - a 17-year-old girl called Carlotta, with more money than sense (a right daddy's girl!) She wants a prom dress.

First they go to Monsoon - Carlotta wanted all the 'cheap' shops out of the way. There was nothing there. Then they travelled in a limo to the designer shops in London. They visited Chanel, Christian Dior, Dolce & Gabbana, Versace, Ralph Lauren and *many* more. Finally, after trying countless numbers of dresses, ridiculously high shoes and *tiny* handbags and eight hours of complaints and moans from Carlotta (some people are so demanding!), they finished with a beautiful dress. It is a Christian Dior, midnight-blue velvet with silver embroidery, costing £165,000, along with blue shoes and a bag.

After Laila is paid, she goes home, has a massaging bath to soak her aching feet and goes to sleep straight away! *Phew* - what a tiring day!

Susannah Tarrant (13)
Rugby High School

The Life Of Billy Jameson, The Premature Baby

Here I am, entangled in wires, draped in electrical devices. These wires are forced up my nostrils. The occasional beeping of many machines is the only sound I hear. Like a mime I am trapped inside a cage of a clear material, unaware of my surroundings. A woman is stroking my hand through a hole in my box, the width of her finger the size of my palm. I can see tears streaming down her face, although she makes no sound. I feel as if all the energy inside of me is gone. I have barely enough energy to breathe. I may have only been alive for twelve hours, but it feels like I have experienced more than anybody, even though I have never felt the sun's rays on my skin, or breathed in the fresh air of the countryside. All I have ever wanted is to live a normal life outside these walls. But I think I shall never be able to do that.

I think I am getting weaker. I can see a screen with green lines moving up and down. They are getting flatter and flatter every second. The woman at my beside places her lips upon my hand, her wet tears trickling on my willowed skin. My lungs are like glass, compressing, making my breath sharper. The woman by my bedside has stood up shouting indistinctly. The green lines are almost flat. I may be too young to understand, but I'm not too young to die.

Sophie Wright (12)
Rugby High School

Bruce

Bruce is my dog. Well, not a dog as such. You see, he's a space dog, from the future. The problem is that when he landed on Earth, he sort of changed. He became invisible.

I know it sounds stupid, right? But it's true. His real name is Brottiart Riacig Uni Carbra Endolyd - Bruce for short. He tells me all of his crazy adventures from his old life and I write them down in books. Maybe you've read one before? I doubt it - my mum says I'm not allowed to print them until I'm grown up.

I know! I'll tell you one of my stories now!

Well, it was a cold, cold night. Bruce sat curled up in his home, when he heard a deep, rumbling noise. Being the curious dog that he is, he went to investigate. He was racing through the town, when he realised the noise had stopped. He looked around and could see nothing at all. Nothing. Just total black.

He felt the ground jerk beneath him. He ran, trying to find something light, anything. Then he saw a long stream of light, fluttering in front of him. He stepped cautiously towards it and closed his eyes as it became blindingly bright. He felt another jerk.

He looked around once more and stared in disbelief at the silver that lay before him. He didn't know where it came from or why, but this was the best day of his life.

Katy Wyton (13)
Rugby High School

A Day In The Life Of A Jew In The Holocaust

'Mummy, *Mummy! Where are you?*' I screamed, looking wildly around me through the crowds of people being herded into the cattle trucks.

'Mary, *Mary!*'

I look in the direction that my name is being called from. I turn round and see my mother racing towards me. Mummy and I never used to be close, but now, she is all I've got. Ever since Father was deported to a Hungarian forced labour camp, it's been just the two of us.

A sudden wave of sadness came over me as I caught sight of the ghetto that had been my home for the past month. That ghetto was the only place I had ever been in my entire life where I felt happy to be a Jew. I felt at home, even though the conditions were awful. It's one of the only places I have ever been where I could mix with Jews my own age. There was nothing to make me stand out as different, a freak. I loved the sense of belonging. But now we had to leave all this behind, be herded on cattle trucks and be taken to an uncertain future that, however, is certain to hold death. Those last few seconds in the ghetto sent a powerful thought through my head. I pictured Aunty Cecelia holding a glass up and proposing a toast. As usual, it was to the future, but this time it was to survival.

Vicki Tomlin (13)
Rugby High School

A Day In The Life Of A Mental Patient

No one believes me. I really did see the day that the world ended, but everyone thinks that I'm psycho. I'll just have to tell you instead. You'll listen, won't you? Of course you will.

Well, I was walking through the streets when a giant flash came from the sky! I fell instantly to the ground. When I finally opened my eyes, I was here. OK, OK, I need to start from the beginning.

I was walking through the blah, blah, blah when I was knocked out. An angel came to me and told me to run as fast as I could on the seventh day of the seventh year, because the sun would explode! Then I went to the future. The sun blew up right there and then, right in front of my eyes.

We travelled back to the day she came to me and when I awoke, she was there. But not as an angel, as a nurse! Am I mad? I must be. Everyone seems to think so, even, well … me! I can't be mad, I just can't. I'm not mad, am I? Do you think I'm mad? Oh dear Lord, please help me, I'm so confused! My life will never be the same, my wife will never love me and my children will have to say, 'Our dad's mental,' and everyone will laugh.

I'm not mental, I won't let that happen. I'm normal I am, just wait, just you wait and see. I'll show you.

Amy Wilson (13)
Rugby High School

The Snow Globe

I have never known my father, as my parents divorced when I was four, ten years ago now. He moved to the opposite side of the Arctic. I've never been able to visit him as the sea has not been hard enough to travel across. Rumour says that this year the sea will be frozen properly for the first time in a decade. I shall go and visit my father with my two brothers, Callum and Doug.

The supplies are packed onto the three skidoos. We are taking our husky, Tinka, with us for company. When we finally set off, Callum spots a storm in the distance and we make haste to find a cave. We find a cave hidden underground with a small skylight in the top.

I've always loved snowstorms; Dad left me a snow globe with a snowstorm swirling around a husky. I watch the snowstorm from the safety of the cave, as I have never watched a snowstorm from underground. I don't understand, it's so beautiful, it's amazing how it rearranges the entire snowy landscape. The storm passes and we continue on our journey. We live like this for several days.

Finally we arrive at a wooden cabin with smoke rising from the chimney. Inside is an older man who looks like an older version of Doug. 'Father,' I cry. He shakes his head and points outside. I see a mound of fresh snow with a wooden cross, and on top lies a snow globe exactly like mine.

Katie Washington (13)
Rugby High School

Untitled

It's all your fault. If you had obeyed - been a good girl - you would not have come to this. You made me do it. Made me stain my hands. These hands that had torn, hacked, screwed at so much. And now they're shaking, right in front of my eyes.

You were my number one. During all those years in solitary confinement, you kept me going. The note, I know it off by heart, despite shredding it in anger after hearing the truth: 'I have faith in you, my love, and I will always be yours. Rachel'.

Well, you can take back your faith, Rachel; it means nothing to me now. I can't afford to pay for all the mistakes you've made, it's about time I claimed the compensation.

It's funny how they dubbed me as 'mentally unstable'. I don't recall ever lying to loved ones, making false promises, elevating someone in such a way - only to smash them to the ground after. Then again, I'm not you.

That's how tonight I found myself face to face with you. The first time in years. Your beautiful face, once passionate towards me, now reflected another lover, and I chuckled as it twisted into something horrible. Something anguished and pain-stricken, as I got my fair share of the deal.

The truth hurts. I'm happy to have shared some of this pain with you. After all, it's only fair. Now excuse me as I wash your blood off my hands.

Beatrice Xu (13)
Rugby High School

A Day In The Life Of Wishful Me

Be careful what you wish for!

I stretched out my arms and slipped on my slippers. I carefully clambered over the piles of clothes on my floor, to my mirror. I peered into the mirror. Where was I? I knew I was there because I could feel myself. I was invisible.

It all started Friday afternoon. I was sitting by the pond when Roxanne came towards me.

'What you lookin' at?' shouted Roxanne in an angry manner. 'Oi, you dissin' me?' she shouted again, getting more frustrated as she spoke. Roxanne looked me up and down. She gave me a kick in the shin and walked away.

After school, I ran home and straight away went to bed, leaving my homework for the morning. I lay in bed and thought, *why won't she leave me alone? They treat me like a piece of dirt. I wish I were invisible.*

And that's what happened. I smiled at my invisible self and the word *'Payback'* flashed in my eyes.

By the end of the day, I had Roxanne in detention for a month, my exam results all As, and a few people with wedgies. It was a great day, but as I lay in bed I thought, *being invisible is good, but I wish I were a dog. Whoops!*

Katie Windridge (13)
Rugby High School

Run!

Her footsteps were fast but quiet as she ran rapidly through the dim and silent streets. Panting, she turned the corner and carried on down the fourth long street she had run down tonight. Worriedly, checking her watch, she quickened her pace again, knowing that if she did not get home soon, it would catch up with her. 'Just concentrate on getting home,' she told herself, 'and then you'll be there soon.'

Suddenly, all the street lamps went out, leaving her drowning in darkness. She tripped, scared, alone and suddenly cold. She sat on the ground, frightened to death. There was a scuffling sound coming from behind the dustbins at the opposite end of the road. *This is it,* she thought, *this is the end.* She closed her eyes, waiting for the attack of the creature that had already killed so many in her town, waiting for its hot breath to surround her, waiting, waiting … but It didn't come. Slowly, she opened her eyes. Horrified, she realised that she was not waiting for the attack of a monster, but a cat. She scrambled up onto her feet, not believing that the monster had not caught up with her yet. She started to run again, this time even more frightened. She turned the final corner, almost home, when she stopped again. The creature was standing right in front of her, its eyes hungry for fresh meat. As it pounced she screamed and then … silence.

Neha Parmar (12)
Rugby High School

Labyrinth

She walked through the pitch-black maze, feeling her way along the winding passages. It was comfortable in the musty darkness - for her at any rate. She was the only one who could enter the deadly labyrinth and not be hopelessly lost, not end up wandering aimlessly around until starvation overcame. She could survive in the weaving web of paths - for she was the one who ruled it and could walk where no others could. But even she had to count the turnings carefully, in case she took the wrong way, in case she walked unwittingly to her death.

She ran her fingers lightly against the wall as she strode along, confident until ... there was no wall. She stopped, hesitant. *Nothing* ever happened in *her* dark domain. Yet here, the wall had been crashed through. Bricks, rubble and dust were heaped on the ground. She stood for a moment, confused and wary. And that was when she heard it. A scraping, slithery sound coming from behind her.

All the monster stories from her childhood came flooding back into her mind instantly. She ran, panicking, forgetting to count the turnings, concentrating on getting away, away from the *thing* behind her.

But her long skirts hampered her. She could not run away. She was lost. And the creature was gaining on her; she could hear its scales rattling, its claws scraping, she could feel its hot breath on her heels ...

No one heard her scream.

Caitlin Spencer (13)
Rugby High School

A Day In The Life Of A Coma Patient

Wake up. Well, I say wake up, but really there's no difference between sleep and consciousness. Motionless. My mind's active, but physically I'm frozen. It's a constant cocoon, hoping someday I'll emerge, but for now I'm just a shell hanging by a thread.

I'm not sure how I got here. For all I know, I could have stepped out in front of a bus, maybe even intentionally. Perhaps I've been here for weeks, months, *years*. I've tried keeping track of time, but the days blur into each other.

There are moments where I'm almost real, like breaking the surface of a swimming pool after holding your breath for too long, fingertips grazing the cold air. But soon enough, I'm back underwater, existing but not living.

When the nausea recedes after times like this, I'm suddenly aware of what could happen to me. I'm not one of those lucky cases. I can't see, can't feel and my hearing is rare. I'm not some Sleeping Beauty, more like a Snow White, trapped inside a glass coffin.

I feel different now. Weirdly out of focus. It's not one of those almost awakenings. It's the same feeling you get after standing up too fast, like turning over an hourglass, all the sand surges to the other side.

And as the usually semi-darkness in front of my eyes starts turning black, there's a sudden rush of senses, the slowing beep of a monitor, a cold hand squeezing mine and the end of a sentence, '… losing her.'

Devawn Wilkinson (13)
Rugby High School

New Wings

One day a long time ago in Fairyland, all the fairies were hiding and peeping out of their windows. It was meant to be the busiest time in Fairyland, well it was, years before the darkest fairy of all the fairies moved to the haunted castle at the top of the hill, overlooking Fairyland. Her name was Katherine.

Katherine was born a young, angelic little fairy. Greed soon took over Katherine's life and when her parents died, she refused to give Fairyland any more money. Soon, her long, golden-blonde hair started to fall out. It grew back short, black and wispy. Her skin began to turn the greyish-green all black fairies' skin goes. Then, one dark winter night, there was a scream and a cloaked person was seen running from Katherine's house. No one saw Katherine for weeks, until one of the bravest farmers decided to walk to the haunted castle and find out what had happened. When he arrived, he tied up the rope and climbed to the only tower with a light. There she was, sitting crying into a picture of her once beautiful face.

When the farmer returned, he told no one that he'd seen Katherine's ugly face and that it was she who lived in the castle.

That night, Katherine left the castle for the first time, with a sharp pole and a sleeping potion. The next day, the farmer's head was found impaled on the pole in the centre of the village.

Hatty Stott (13)
Rugby High School

Fire Starter

She ran and ran, struggling through the trees and panting at the strain of uphill running. She stopped at the top of the hill and stood among the trees. She watched the flames from the roof igniting the sky, their smouldering colours etching themselves into the inky-blue background. The smell of smoke stuck to her like incense and she loved it. She closed her eyes and smiled.

He had seen her do all this, watching like some kind of stalker. He had seen her heading towards the old house in the dell and reach gingerly into her school bag, and draw out the can of petrol. He had heard the glug of the petrol as she poured it in a steady stream through the house and over the old, dusty furnishings. He had tasted the sweat dripping from his forehead in anticipation and noted that she too was sweating as she retrieved a lighter from her bag. He had felt the same rush of adrenaline as she dropped the lighter on the end of the petrol trail and it burned its way into the house. But, most importantly, he too had the incense smell of smoke.

Amelia Walsh (13)
Rugby High School

A Day In The Life Of A Penny

That 99p ruler. That's how I was first used. A little girl who paid with a pound coin and was excited when she got me as her change. But I'm not as good as paper? Those notes are so much better than we pennies, aren't they? And they don't half show it.

Every day I am passed from pocket to pocket, purse to purse, without a care in the world. Oh! Who is this, I wonder? Nice house, is that a gold necklace I see? Here we go again. Hand comes in the pocket, coin comes out. Hand comes in the pocket, *tissue* comes out. Wait! I'm stuck! Help, help! Ow! On the ground, that's great. I might as well have a sign on my head saying, *Stand Here*. Yeah, you can pick me up again now! Or not! That's it, you just walk off. I'm worthless, aren't I? Rich people don't need us pennies! Who are you? It's another *'See a penny, pick it up, all day you'll have good luck'* person. That's right, you drop me. Yep! I was right back on the floor. This is my future. On the floor for the rest of my life.

Hello, you seem nice. Yuck! You smell a bit. Those clothes aren't the nicest I've seen. And, no gold necklace. Well I suppose that's a good sign. Oh, you're that man who lives on the streets, aren't you! You actually need me!

Florence Thornton-Weeks (12)
Rugby High School

Helpline

I am here again.

As I walk, the stench rises towards me as I unsettle years of grime that has soaked into the carpet. It was once white and pure, but now it is darkened with decay.

I am here again.

I reach for the telephone and pick it up. I know the number off by heart. It was my comfort whilst I stroked the sore, sore bruises that he tattooed on my body with his fists.

I am here again.

The phone rings. There is a noise as someone picks up the receiver. A key scrapes in the lock. He's here. I drop the phone with a clatter, but he's already through the door. His eyes rage with fire. A voice rings clearly from the phone, 'Child Helpline,' it calls. He reels towards me.

I am here again.

I wake up screaming, but Helen is already here, wrapping her warm, safe arms around me. They say she is my guardian. Is she an angel? She already knows what I have been dreaming of.

I can only remember pain. I still bear the scars; they will always be etched on my face.

I visited my father in prison today. I think he tried to smile at me, but his eyes were empty. They are no longer on fire. They are cold, so cold. It makes me afraid. Helen squeezes my hand.

She is always there.

Jennifer Simmons (13)
Rugby High School

The Unsinkable

As Sephina, our submarine, moves closer to the sunken wreck of the Titanic, several objects come into view. Our digital camera moves closer. The objects are becoming clearer and clearer. They look like items from a first class bedroom. There is a shoe, a dress and an expensive-looking pen. The shoe is very small; leather, with intricate designs stitched on. It must have belonged to a very young child. As our image becomes more focused, it is almost as if I am going back in time ...

'Come along, Idylle, you don't want to be late for our evening meal now, do you?'

'Wait a minute, Mother, my shoe keeps coming undone.'

As her mother waited impatiently, Idylle bent down to tie her shoelace, her face red with concentration. She then quickly hurried after her mother, trying to get through the tangle of dirty, smelly third class passengers.

'Mother, help me!'

'What now?'

'This shoe keeps falling off!'

'Oh come on, dear, we shall be late! You will be changing into your evening dress soon, anyway.'

Idylle struggled on valiantly. She knew she must make good time for dinner, shoe or no shoe. And she was very fortunate indeed to be travelling on such a great, unsinkable ship as the Titanic ...

As more objects come into focus, I fall silent. I am an eyewitness to the remains of one of history's great tragedies.

Charlotte Wild (13)
Rugby High School

Wings

Felix had always dreamed that he would have friends. Proper friends. Friends that wouldn't tease him. Was that really possible?

Felix was very interested in mythology. He had been all his life; particularly myths that included winged animals. For this, his 'friends' were always teasing him for liking animals that had wings, real or mythical. So it was only to be expected that, when he appeared at the school canteen armed with a book containing stories of ancient elf-fairies that cast spells by chanting haiku, they howled with laughter.

'Come on then, Fee-fee, what fairy tale are you reading today?'

'It isn't girly,' Felix defended.

'Go on then, read us a really manly part to prove your point.'

Felix hesitated. If he didn't read an extract, they would think he was reading girly books. He sighed, then put the book on the table in front of him, letting it fall open to the page his bookmark was poking out from at the top.

'Oh, it's a spell book.' The bully was delighted. He read aloud,

'Give him wings to fly,
Through all forests, caves and sky,
'Til the day he dies'.

All at once, a shower of sparks erupted from the book. Screams rang around the canteen, and wings sprouted from Felix's back. Wings! He had wings!

'Stay back,' he yelled, 'or I'll do the same to you! These books have meanings!'

And they stayed back. And have done since then, leaving Felix to lead his extraordinary new life with real, trusting friends.

Katy Outhwaite (12)
Rugby High School

A Trip To Google Land

There I was, cleaning out the rabbit's cage for Simba, my rabbit, when it happened. Suddenly, I blanked out and hit something hard. It was a shining blue portal. My mind went blank and I just wanted to enter. When I approached the portal, it sucked me and my rabbit slowly up.

On the other side of the portal it was fantastic. There was pink grass and golden trees with muddy leaves, as well as silver palaces and prickly mountains.

As I explored, I felt something hard around the rocks. It felt different this time. It was my rabbit, Simba.

I could see the portal beginning to close. I grabbed Simba and threw him in the portal. The portal closed on me and I began to cry. I was trapped!

Suddenly, a dragon appeared in front of me. I had a look at the dragon. I could see that she was crying too. She looked at me with her red, cat eyes. As I went closer to her, I could see a piece of goblin bone under her foot. Under the bone was another portal. I ran up to the foot and I jumped for it. The dragon looked at me again and I thought that she was going to eat me, but she said, 'Come back any time you want!'

So I came back, every month.

William Henstone (13)
The Round Oak School & Support Service

A Trip To Dream World

(An extract)

I was in my bedroom looking for some paper with my friends, when I moved my printer and found a hole the size of a fox.

The hole under my computer desk was as black as mud. I could see a lovely light shining at the end. I began to crawl slowly towards the light. The tunnel was icy cold, like a freezer. I felt I was in the tunnel for a week, but I wasn't - I was only in there for an hour.

Suddenly, I was on top of a chocolate mountain. It tasted lovely! As I looked down, I could see in the distance a wonderful waterfall made out of Smarties. There were pink flowers made out of marshmallow. They smelt sweet and lovely, and the flowers felt soft as a bunny rabbit's fur.

In the middle of the trees there was a pretty pond with chocolate frogs leaping about. The sky was as green as grass. The rainbow birds fluttered by, singing their sweet songs.

I was taking in the scenery when suddenly the ground around me shook. In front of me was and enormous dragon! The dragon had one enormous green-yellow eye in the middle of his scaly forehead. His nose was shaped like a pen. He had long, sharp claws and scales all over his feet. The beast had wings like a bird's, that flapped furiously in the air. The dragon was electric-blue in colour. He had three sharp, unicorn-like horns. The beast had ears like tall, pointed towers in a castle. His tale was long and leathery.

Shantelle (14)
The Round Oak School & Support Service

Candy Land

I was playing with my dog when his ball went under my bed. I put my hand under the bed and me and my dog were sucked into a hole. My dog barked and we were gone.

When I came round, I was in the bed with my dog, but we were in a strange place. We were both scared. We fell off the bed and landed in a chocolate river. We swam in it and ate the chocolate. We were under a chocolate waterfall and it was lovely.

We landed on the bank and then a strange creature came up to me and started to talk. 'Hello, my name is Candy.'

Candy was made out of Smarties and had strawberry laces for hair. She flapped her wings and landed on the creamy ground beside me. We ate the delicious sweets around us.

I jumped on the pink candyfloss clouds. I landed on a flying rock, which flew everywhere, and Candy flew behind me. My dog licked his lips and ate the chocolate. Candy told me that chocolate snowflakes fell down from the sky every night. I wished I could stay in Candy Land forever.

Then I saw my bed with the portal to go home, but Candy wouldn't let me go. I had to make a choice: to go home, or stay in Candy Land.

I decided that I'd better go home because my mum would be wondering where I was. But I came back every day through the portal under my bed, to be in Candy heaven!

Rebecca Sokoroniec (13)
The Round Oak School & Support Service

Love Land

(An extract)

It all happened when I was in my room. I was playing with my hamster when all of a sudden it bit me for no reason. Why did it bite me? Before I could figure it out, I fell on the floor. I was as small as a tiny, weeny little mouse. My mom came in and saw me like a mouse, and hit me with a broom. I ran as fast as I could, and ran in a mouse hole.

I was in another world, with lots of animals. There was a signpost above me, it said 'Love Land'. A unicorn came up to me and said, 'Hello! My name is Milly. Nice to meet you. Let me show you around Love Land.'

It was an enormous place, with lots of animals of all kinds. Clouds were as golden as a royal palace. There was sky as blue as bluebells. I could see fairies flying and swooping in the sky like aeroplanes. Flying dolphins flew in the sky, then splashed into the ocean, like mermaids swimming by. Couples everywhere were kissing like fish. When I finished my tour, I could see in the distance a figure of a half dragon, half man ...

Caroline Day (13)
The Round Oak School & Support Service

Dragonant And The Giant Peach

One sunny day I was in the garden with my friends and I saw a beautiful peach. I walked over to touch the peach and I saw a little door. I began to shrink to the size of a small child.

The journey was very rough a I walked through the peach. There was a sweet, gorgeous smell that made me feel hungry. The orange walls felt slimy and soggy. I started to walk slowly, but I was sticking to the floor. The floor felt all spongy and soft. I took each step, carefully, until I came to the middle. All I could see was orange walls everywhere. I started to go deeper and deeper down into the lush juice and I saw a funny creature; it was a dragonant. He walked towards me with a grumpy look on his face. Dragonant was thin and stringy. He moved as slowly as a hedgehog. He had a bright pink, black and red body that glowed in the dark. His eyes were red, like a dragon's. I turned and ran away as fast as I could. I came to a door and went outside to lay on the grass. I shut my eyes and realised it was all a dream.

Christopher Cooper (13)
The Round Oak School & Support Service